BEATING BIPOLAR

HAY HOUSE TITLES OF RELATED INTEREST

YOU CAN HEAL YOUR LIFE, the movie, starring Louise L. Hay & Friends
(available as a 1-DVD program and an expanded 2-DVD set)
Watch the trailer at: **www.LouiseHayMovie.com**

THE SHIFT, the movie, starring Dr. Wayne W. Dyer
(available as a 1-DVD program and an expanded 2-DVD set)
Watch the trailer at: **www.DyerMovie.com**

●　　●　　●

ANXIETY FREE: Unravel Your Fears Before They Unravel You
and
BEAT THE BLUES BEFORE THEY BEAT YOU: How to Overcome Depression,
by Robert L. Leahy, Ph.D.

*DEFENDERS OF THE HEART: Managing the Habits and
Attitudes That Block You from a Richer, More Satisfying Life,*
by Marilyn Kagan, LCSW, and Neil Einbund Ph.D.

*THE EYES OF FAITH: How to Not Go Crazy: Thoughts to Bear in Mind to Get
Through Even the Worst Days,* by Ben Stein

JOINING FORCES: Empowering Male Survivors to Thrive, by Dr. Howard Fradkin

NO STORM LASTS FOREVER: Transforming Suffering Into Insight,
by Dr. Terry A. Gordon

*10 STEPS TO TAKE CHARGE OF YOUR EMOTIONAL LIFE: Overcoming Anxiety,
Distress, and Depression Through Whole-Person Healing,* by Eve A. Wood, M.D.

All of the above are available at your local bookstore, or may be
ordered by visiting:

Hay House USA: **www.hayhouse.com**®
Hay House Australia: **www.hayhouse.com.au**
Hay House UK: **www.hayhouse.co.uk**
Hay House South Africa: **www.hayhouse.co.za**
Hay House India: **www.hayhouse.co.in**

BEATING BIPOLAR

HOW ONE THERAPIST TACKLED HIS ILLNESS . . .
AND HOW WHAT HE LEARNED COULD HELP YOU!

BLAKE LEVINE

INSIGHTS

HAY HOUSE, INC.
Carlsbad, California • New York City
London • Sydney • Johannesburg
Vancouver • Hong Kong • New Delhi

Published and distributed in the United States by: Hay House, Inc.: www.hay house.com® • *Published and distributed in Australia by:* Hay House Australia Pty. Ltd.: www.hayhouse.com.au • *Published and distributed in the United Kingdom by:* Hay House UK, Ltd.: www.hayhouse.co.uk • *Published and distributed in the Republic of South Africa by:* Hay House SA (Pty), Ltd.: www .hayhouse.co.za • *Distributed in Canada by:* Raincoast: www.raincoast.com • *Published in India by:* Hay House Publishers India: www.hayhouse.co.in

Cover design: Jason Harvey • *Interior design:* Jenny Richards

Library of Congress Cataloging-in-Publication Data

LeVine, Blake.
  Beating bipolar : how one therapist tackled his illness-- and how what he learned could help you! / Blake LeVine. -- 1st ed.
    p. cm.
  ISBN 978-1-4019-3951-9 (tradepaper : alk. paper)
  1. Manic-depressive illness--Treatment--Popular works. 2. Mental illness--Psychological aspects. 3. Self-care, Health--Popular works. I. Title.
  RC516.L48 2012
  616.89'5--dc23
                                    2012019228

Tradepaper ISBN: 978-1-4019-3951-9
Digital ISBN: 978-1-4019-3952-6

15 14 13 12   4 3 2 1
1st edition, November 2012

FSC
www.fsc.org
MIX
Paper from
responsible sources
FSC® C011935

I dedicate <u>Beating Bipolar</u> to the two lights of my life: my wife, Jennifer, and our daughter, Tyler. They demonstrate to me every day why I want to stay in recovery. I also dedicate this book to the many other people who have contributed to my wellness and sanity, particularly my parents, brother and sisters, friends, and mental health partners. You've not only guided and cheered me in my continued growth, but have also been great examples of how to live a healthy and joyous life. To my clients, thank you for showing me true grit. Your determination has been a never-ending source of inspiration. Be proud of your progress!

CONTENTS

INTRODUCTION

IF YOU'RE READING these words, you're likely affected in some way by *bipolar disorder*. You or someone close to you has experienced the hyper-frenzied highs, paralyzing lows, and periods of normalcy that mark the condition once referred to commonly as *manic depression*. You understand or have some awareness of the devastation that these episodes can wreak in terms of failed relationships, financial disasters, and other ruinous behaviors in your life.

Not that you need a reminder, but when mania takes hold, it can prompt the most indiscriminate and uncharacteristic sexual—and even criminal—behavior and substance abuse imaginable. Self-criticism, self-control, and the ability to self-judge go out the window. You're left with a volatile combination of excessive self-confidence and self-esteem, fueled by unbridled energy, a lack of inhibition, and too little sleep. During manic episodes, you sense that you can take on the world.

Conversely, when depressive episodes take charge, they can drag your life into slow motion, robbing you of your energy; initiative; and ability to think, move, and process memory or ideas. This can erode your self-confidence and weigh you down with such guilt and despair that you can't take on the trivial stuff, let alone big obstacles. It's too difficult to make and keep friends. Sleep is a preferred companion. And at your lowest of low moments, you may even contemplate or attempt suicide, the tragic choice of last resort.

It's crushing to admit that this is your life or that of someone you love. *Beating Bipolar* is intended to offer you hope, encouragement, and support. Whether you have accepted your diagnosis and are on the path to recovery and restored health, or are a neophyte in coming to grips with your mental illness, I'm confident that you'll gain much from this book. If someone you care about has these symptoms, you'll also gain insight and perspective. Although *Beating Bipolar* addresses sufferers specifically, the advice is intended for a wider audience of friends, family members, and others who may feel helpless and scared. If you're related to or advocating for someone with this disorder, I pray that you'll keep up your support.

No matter what your role, it's my wish that you'll find help and encouragement in the simple strategies that have worked for my clients—and yes, *me*. Although I've counseled countless bipolar individuals as both a social worker and life coach, I'm more than just an objective observer of this mental illness. I, too, have lived with, been challenged by, and sometimes even *fought* this disease. I've also gained immensely from it. This book is a teaching tool. It's a compilation of things I've learned that may help you handle your symptoms and reach your highest potential.

It's my earnest hope that when you appreciate the therapeutic reasons for getting an accurate diagnosis and participating in the right treatment, you'll accept your illness and move forward with purpose and vigor. To help you with the process, I've divided this book into four easy-to-navigate parts:

Part I: Unraveling Bipolar. In Chapter 1, I share my bipolar story. Although the facts may sound all too familiar if you've been in crisis or have witnessed it in loved ones, you'll understand why I'm driven to help others. I also cover basics about this disorder, including the potential episodic triggers. Chapter 2 discusses the tools and criteria psychiatrists use to diagnose bipolar disorder, especially in identifying the four distinct types of this condition. I'll also explain why you need to be diagnosed officially to have any hope of dealing with your illness effectively.

Part II: Tackling Your Illness. Chapter 3 delves into the challenges you face as a bipolar individual and tells you why they're not (I repeat, *not*) insurmountable. Also examined are the manifestations of this disorder so that you'll know what to look for in yourself or others.

Chapters 4, 5, and 6 target specific therapies worth pursuing in overcoming your illness. The good news is that today's treatment approaches are very effective not only in physiologically controlling manic and depressive episodes, but also in helping you understand any underlying issues or behaviors. I offer techniques to positively release your manic energy and lessen your depression so you can live on a normal, even keel.

Part III: Cementing Relationships, Both Old and New. Chapter 7 examines the many ways in which you can break the isolation of your illness and find new avenues for healthy relationships. Chapter 8 looks at the challenges of finding romance and love when you have a mental illness. As I demonstrate, it can be done!

Part IV: Mapping a New Life. In Chapter 9, we explore the power of persistence and hope in dealing with your bipolar disorder. I tell you why you need to take time and have faith that you can accomplish great things. Chapter 10 demonstrates the joys of pursuing new adventures as a healthier individual. Entire worlds can open up for you.

You may already be versed in some of the tools and techniques that I discuss in this book. Then again, others will likely be unfamiliar to you. But I believe that when you're dealing with a chronic mental illness, you can never have too much information or hear the message too often. Even if you glean only one new idea from *Beating Bipolar,* you're one new idea closer to living healthy and fulfilled.

I hope that in the process, you realize that you don't have to be ashamed of your illness. Those of us who are controlling our bipolar have proven that we're not such a danger to society that we need to be locked away. As more of us make positive contributions to the community, we demonstrate that being susceptible to mania and depression doesn't mean permanent hospitalization or deteriorating mental wellness. With today's treatments, you can master this chronic illness. You can live, work, and love just as your family, friends, and neighbors do.

In fact, throughout this book I'll share my past struggles and those of others who are now living free of symptoms. I like to think that we're not only living healthy, but also serving as beacons to the world. By taking responsibility and an active role in our own recovery, we light a path for other bipolar individuals and supporters. More important, we dispel the myths about our illness and educate the public as to its realities.

My hope is that *Beating Bipolar* will empower you to take crucial steps toward your own good health. I believe fervently that you can do it!

•   •   •

PART I

UNRAVELING
BIPOLAR

Note: Many of the stories in this book are true accounts in which the names and identifying details have been changed to protect confidentiality. Others are composites drawn from years of clinical work. The latter are true to the spirit of teaching, although not to the experience of any particular person.

CHAPTER ONE

INTO THE LIGHT

MY LIFE IS like that of many Americans. If you met me, you'd encounter a happy, measured individual who loves his work and adores his beautiful wife, Jennifer, and our precocious daughter, Tyler. I'm a therapist, life coach, public speaker, and author. I enjoy wide-ranging interests and many loyal friends. By every measure, I've achieved success. You could even say I'm living the American dream.

I'm also living successfully with bipolar disorder. I'm able to experience the wonders of the world around me, because I control my illness. It no longer controls me. I have no delusions, figuratively or otherwise. To remain stable, I know I must take care of myself both physically and emotionally. I stay on a prescription regimen. I maintain a healthy diet and lifestyle. I do everything in my power to balance my moods so that I'm not shifting from the abnormal highs to the abnormal lows that defined my youth.

I've come a long way since I was first diagnosed at age 15. My personal journey with this disorder has been filled with messy twists and turns. As anyone who suffers from a mental illness understands, it dramatically impacts not only those living with it but everyone in his or her sphere. That's me. That's my family. I've witnessed the darkest sides of bipolar disorder, particularly the mania, but I know that with treatment you can experience light. After more than 15 years of nearly perfect health, without a manic or depressive episode, I'm proof that there's hope for those of us living with this mental illness.

You may wonder why I'm telling my story. This book is not about just surviving; it's about *thriving*. It's about arming yourself with information and pulling together practical strategies for navigating an illness that doesn't have to rule your life. I've seen the positive results from medications and therapy. I've worked with clients who have made so much progress with this illness that they're functioning like friends and neighbors who aren't saddled with a mental disease. They've blossomed into healthy, participating adults who have developed relationships, contributed their talents, and accomplished their dreams.

But we all have one thing in common; Those of us who have carved out healthy lives work at it each day. We're well aware of how bipolar can zap your energy and mess around with your head. We also know that there's often no straight line between diagnosis and the best treatment plan. There are many ups and downs . . . hits and misses . . . in finding solutions.

Yet, like us, when you choose to understand, accept, and otherwise overcome the challenges of bipolar disorder, the rewards are many. When you decide it's worth your time, peace of mind, and future happiness to come to grips with your illness by seeking treatment, the payoff will be immense. You'll be stronger when you're in control of your illness. You'll be healthier when you've balanced your moods to stay sane. You'll be poised to rebuild your life with inner calm, peace, and joy, because you will no longer have the emotional baggage of your illness or past weighing you down.

That's not to say that you'll be free of grief or problems. Just because you experience measurable relief doesn't mean you'll have clear sailing. Life doesn't work that way. But when you view bipolar disorder as an opportunity, rather than an albatross, you're free to examine *who* you are and *where* you want to go from this moment forward. You lay the groundwork for many positive consequences: improved relationships, wiser choices, and the capacity to be courageous and confident.

When you take charge, you're no longer on autopilot. What do I mean by that? Well, you're not just going through the motions of living, because some faulty mechanism inside your brain is driving you to think and do crazy or strange things. You're piloting your own life. No matter what inner struggles you face, no matter where you are in your journey, it is within your ability to call the shots and be comfortable with the outcomes.

So now is not the time to retreat. Now is the time to be bold, brave, and open to a wonderful transformation. If you haven't already experienced change with your mental illness, you may wonder how you can ever achieve it. You start by knowing your disease and then taking advantage of the strategies I've outlined in *Beating Bipolar*. They include the many tools that modern medicine and psychotherapy offer today that weren't available years ago. By being diagnosed officially, treated effectively, and open to the support of others, you *can* make dramatic changes in your life.

Although you've been laboring under the cloud of a debilitating illness, rest assured that the sun is about to shine. I'm not just offering you pie-in-the-sky platitudes about realizing lofty goals. I truly believe that you can be healthier and happier than you are right now. Once you're no longer dealing with the self-destructive highs of mania or the suicidal lows of depression, you can embrace the moment. You can plan for the future. By opening your mind to healing, you'll move from darkness into light! That's what I did!

You Aren't Alone

When I was first diagnosed, there were very few role models sharing their struggles with bipolar disorder. I read actress Patty Duke's revealing book *A Brilliant Madness: Living with Manic-Depressive Illness*. Although it covered bipolar in great detail, I still didn't know another young person who had dealt with, much less overcome, this disorder.

Thankfully, today I have a much better appreciation of both my condition and my fellow travelers. Mental illnesses touch nearly every individual in that most of us have a friend, relative, or acquaintance facing this challenge. Some six million adult Americans, or 2.6 percent of people aged 18 or older, are affected by bipolar disorder every year, according to the Depression and Bipolar Support Alliance (DBSA), a leading advocacy organization for sufferers of these mood disorders. The median age of onset is 25, even though bipolar can appear as early as childhood or the teenage years, as it did for me, or as late as your 40s and 50s.[1] Recent studies suggest that the incidence could be as high as 1 percent in children and adolescents, even though controversy exists over the criteria used to accurately diagnose younger people.[2]

In any case, bipolar disorder is an equal-opportunity problem in terms of race, social class, gender, and profession. Those of us with this mental illness are working as teachers, therapists, doctors, firefighters, truck drivers, and nurses. We're husbands, wives, mentors, and great friends. We share this illness with an impressive array of luminaries in music, science, mathematics, politics, the arts, and other disciplines.

Obviously, we can't go back in time to diagnose people who have long since left us. But that hasn't prevented some scientists from speculating that a multitude of historical figures may have suffered from what is today known as *bipolar disorder.* Short-story writer and poet Edgar Allan Poe and First Lady Mary Todd Lincoln, for instance, are among a long list of creative types and other celebrated figures known—from letters, contemporaneous accounts, or other anecdotal material—to have experienced manic or depressive symptoms, even though none of them carried the specter of "bipolar disorder."

We have much better luck in identifying recent sufferers, in part because they mention their diagnosis in memoirs, interviews, and other very public conversations. Among a second long list of living luminaries, actress Carrie Fisher, author Patricia Cornwell, and political activist Patrick J. Kennedy have shared their personal struggles and triumphs in overcoming this disease.

Actress Catherine Zeta-Jones, for instance, revealed her own bipolar II–related depression during turbulent family times. She went public while also dealing with the throat cancer of her husband, actor Michael Douglas, and her stepson's drug conviction. By balancing her treatment with family and work obligations, however, Zeta-Jones demonstrated that you can navigate this condition and other life hurdles with strength and grace.

Similarly, actress/singer Demi Lovato was admitted to rehab for her battles with bulimia, anorexia, self-mutilation, and depression. After facing the reality that her issues also included bipolar disorder, Lovato decided to share her struggles and road to recovery with millions of other young women, many of whom know her as a Disney star. By going public with her illness, Lovato hopes to be a role model for others facing similar mental health issues. She, too, is proving that you can have a great, productive life, despite having a mental illness.

Are Creative Types Prone to Bipolar Disorder?

There's no question that many of the creative individuals behind the films we watch, the songs we sing, the books we read, and the inventions we use today have suffered from bipolar disorder. But does that necessarily mean that this mental illness occurs more often in people with artistic talent or even high IQs? The great Greek thinkers might have thought so. Although Plato and Socrates make mention of poets and priests communicating with the gods through divine or inspired "madness," Aristotle was the first to suggest a tie between *melancholia,* the ancient forerunner of depression, and the gifted.

Today's scientists are grappling with pinpointing the potential links between creative genius and mental illness, even though, for some researchers, the relationship is indisputable. In her 1993 book, *Touched with Fire: Manic-Depressive Illness and the Artistic Temperament*, Johns Hopkins University School of Medicine clinical psychologist Kay Redfield Jamison, Ph.D., argues that bipolar and other mood disorders may be found in a disproportionately high number of creative professionals, such as actors, artists, comedians, musicians, authors, performers, and poets.

To make her case for the correlation between artistic temperament and mania or depression, Jamison relied on *biographical* or *posthumous research.* That is, she delved into the lives of history's greatest creative figures, combining her own review of anecdotal and other evidence about their symptoms with a spate of scientific studies, conducted through the centuries, suggesting the link. Among the luminaries Jamison cites to prove her thesis are author Herman Melville, artist Vincent van Gogh, and composer Robert Schumann.

Other scientists agree that bipolar disorder and creativity go hand in hand. One theory suggests that the altered chemical balance within the brain actually liberates people during mania to be their creative best. It frees them to write, paint, compose, or otherwise create with heightened sensitivity and awareness, and the deepest of emotions. During depression it allows them to reach into the very depths of their souls to unleash their creativity in resonating and innovative ways.

The jury is still out on the existence of such links for other, skeptical scientists who await better research evidence of how artistic temperament, personality, and other factors figure into the equation.[3]

Whatever forces are at work, being bipolar doesn't mean you're automatically gifted musically, artistically, or with words—far from it. Even Jamison admits that not everyone with bipolar will be an artistic superstar or inventive whiz kid. We're not all destined to be creative geniuses. In fact, most individuals with bipolar aren't overly creative, and most creative people don't suffer from bipolar or any other mental health challenge. Obviously other talents, cognitive capabilities, intuitive traits, and passions come into play.

But by channeling your energies toward *your* dreams and goals, you can achieve success, perhaps even greatness, in your chosen field. You have the ability to create something outstanding in your life. Your special role may not be on the public stage, but by becoming healthy, you, too, can be successful. Whether you're an innovator or builder, thinker or doer, you can make your mark on the world.

. . . .

Genes, the Brain, and Other Factors

So how is it that some of us are afflicted with bipolar disorder, and so many others are not? Although scientists are still probing the intricacies of this mental illness, they're certain that many factors, rather than just one, are working together to either cause the illness or intensify the symptoms. Research to date points to a complex matrix of both internal and external factors, and physiological and psychological triggers. Even though the picture is far from complete, what scientists have learned thus far is helping doctors diagnose and treat this mental illness. That's critical to you in your personal journey with this disease. Perhaps you're already aware of possible mechanisms behind your bipolar, but if not, consider what might be in play in *you:*

— **Brain function and metabolism differences.** High-tech imaging tools, such as *functional magnetic resonance imaging* (fMRI) and *positron emission tomography* (PET) scanners, have given scientists a remarkable opportunity to peer inside and study the living brain. In so doing, they've discovered that there may be subtle structural and functional differences in the brains of bipolar sufferers versus healthy people or individuals with other mental illnesses.[4, 5]

One study, for instance, found a similarity in the brain patterns of children suffering from bipolar disorder and those with *multidimensional impairment,* a condition that produces symptoms overlapping with both bipolar and schizophrenia. These pattern similarities suggest a possible link between unstable moods and specific brain development.[6]

Scientists also made other compelling discoveries concerning certain couriers or chemical messengers called *neurotransmitters,* which ferry instructions between nerve cells. By telling a receiving cell to do or not do something, they trigger and control a host of brain and body functions, including moods, anxiety, impulsivity, fear, sexual activity, and sleep. Researchers believe there's a link between messengers such as *serotonin, dopamine,* and *noradrenaline (norepinephrine),* and mood disorders.[7] (They've been led down this investigative path, in part, because drugs that alter neurotransmitters have been successful in relieving mood disorders.) Some studies have suggested that excesses, deficiencies, or imbalances among these specific chemicals and hormones may be driving the various characteristic highs, lows, and in-between mood states of bipolar disorder. Others have found evidence that a change in the sensitivity of the receptors on nerve cells could be a factor.[8]

We have yet to understand all of the machinations of the brain in terms of bipolar disorder, including the way it processes and uses these and other targeted chemicals, such as *glutamate* and *GABA* (*gamma-aminobutyric acid*). But by deciphering these functions, in addition to the role of genetics, scientists may one day be able to help physicians predict which treatment will work the best on bipolar patients. Trial and error may be a thing of the past.

In the meantime, many of us are benefiting from a bevy of prescription drugs that correct the brain's faulty chemical messengers so that we behave normally. They're the reason we can achieve sanity. The promising news is that new and better ways to live stable and restored may be on the horizon. Scientists just have to find them.

— **Genetics.** Because bipolar disorder seems to run in families, scientists are hunting feverishly for the *genes* that may increase someone's chance of developing this disease. As the "building blocks" of heredity, genes contain every piece of information your body needs to work and grow. They're passed down from generation to generation and stored in millions upon millions of your cells. Genes are the reason why we look and behave like our parents and grandparents. In the case of bipolar disorder, they're also the reason why children with an affected parent or sibling are four to six times more likely to develop the illness than children who don't have a bipolar family member or family history.[9] More than two-thirds of bipolar disorder sufferers have at least one close blood relative with the illness or major depression. One such parent puts the risk for each child at 15 to 30 percent. Both such parents increase the probability to the range of 50 to 75 percent.[10]

Technology is facilitating the work of scientists in decoding the role of genetics for all mental illnesses. The Bipolar Disorder Phenome Database, funded in part by the National Institute of Mental Health (NIMH), is one example of the advances. By tapping into this bank of extensive information, researchers have been able to link visible signs of the disorder with specific genes that might influence its expression.[11]

They've learned, for instance, that most bipolar disorder sufferers not only have been hospitalized for their condition but also are likely to experience other health issues, such as panic disorders and alcohol or substance abuse. Researchers also have discovered certain bipolar family traits: a history of psychiatric hospitalizations, co-occurring obsessive-compulsive disorder, and similar experiences with both the frequency and onset of manic episodes. Although genes seem to be at work, they aren't the only factors. Several identical-twin studies have shown that even if one twin has bipolar disorder, the other won't necessarily develop it. The more likely scenario is that a person's environment and additional genes play a part.

Scientists still don't fully grasp how these factors come together or how family traits fit into the overall picture with genes. But they hope that further investigation will lead to a better understanding of the causes, treatment, and even prevention.[12] In the meantime, if your doctor knows that a blood relative has had a similar mental illness, he or she will look closely at bipolar disorder as a possible diagnosis.

— **Other issues.** Studies have shown that people with bipolar also may suffer from conditions that are sometimes confusingly similar: anxiety disorders (such as post-traumatic stress disorder, or PTSD; attention deficit disorder, or ADD; and attention deficit/hyperactivity disorder, or ADHD). They're also prone to an array of health issues, including migraine headaches, diabetes, obesity, and thyroid or heart disease. Many bipolar individuals also have problems with alcohol and substance abuse. Although scientists aren't completely certain of the reasons for these links, they know that trying to mask your symptoms via addiction can only prolong or intensify your episodes.

— **Major outside triggers.** Evidence consistently shows that factors such as stress and past traumas can also have a bearing on this illness. One-third to one-half of individuals diagnosed with bipolar later in life can point to a traumatic or abusive experience earlier, while they were growing up.[13] These findings suggest that the human brain may have the capacity to change physiologically in reaction to a severe ordeal or loss at a critical age. The alterations, in turn, may influence how the brain regulates mood, making people more susceptible to elation and sadness. Not surprisingly, there's also evidence that recent life events can prompt bipolar onset and recurrence, just as they do in normal depression.[14]

A Tempest in My Head

While scientists sort out the riddle, those of us who actually suffer from bipolar disorder are *living* the puzzle. When you read my story, for instance, you're likely to nod in agreement now and again, because you'll probably recognize bits and pieces of your own story in the ordeal that led me to an accurate diagnosis, successful treatment, and a happy adulthood. Yet I believe it's important to share how I transitioned from those troubled years to today. Just as I've gained perspective on my life, I hope that my familiarity with this illness, which I detail below and throughout this book, will help you gain perspective on *your* life. Rest assured, we're all in this together!

In the Beginning

My experience with bipolar disorder certainly didn't start the day I heard my diagnosis. That's not surprising, since many of us have a convoluted history with this disorder. My symptoms surfaced long before doctors accurately identified their source. (As I discuss later, pinpointing this condition in young people is particularly challenging.) I believe that events far back in my past laid the groundwork for a lifelong condition that finally emerged in its entire scary splendor at age 15.

If there really is a link between early life events and this illness, I can attest to it. I was traumatized at age three by my parents' nasty divorce. It not only tore our family apart, but also took me away from my mother for ten months. She had been granted full custody, leaving my father with limited, supervised visitation rights. Angry, depressed, and hurt, he hired someone to snatch me off the street, while my mother and her friend watched in disbelief. The man literally knocked my mom to the ground, picked me up, and threw me into the car with my father.

During the following months, I ached to see my mother. Even though my dad was kind to me, he only allowed me to talk to her once in a while. She'd scream into the phone, "Blake, where are you?" All I could say was, "I'm in the green house down the street. Please come see me." I was so sad when she didn't rescue me. But I was too young to realize that my father had taken me hundreds of miles from my home in New York—to South Carolina. I lived in a green house all right, but it definitely wasn't down the street. Fortunately, my mother eventually found me. Reuniting with her was one of the most joyous times of my life. She even found the strength to forgive my father, partly because she knew that he loved me greatly.

My dad and I enjoy a strong relationship today. Yet the pain of that experience was etched into every fiber of my being. I lost the confidence and security that children usually develop from sensing that their parents have a loving, stable relationship. It was ripped from me. Losing contact with my mother, even for several months, was devastating.

Whatever role my abduction had in my bipolar, it certainly left me with a high level of insecurity and the need to accomplish much to shield myself from deep emotional wounds. For much of the next decade I pushed myself to the limits to produce, produce, and produce. I can't help but believe that those of us who suffer bipolar disorder are definitely reaping what was sown in our past.

Moving Toward the Cliff

My abduction may have set the stage, but it would be another 12 years before I exhibited manic behavior so bizarre that my mother had to call in the doctors. From late childhood into my midteens, I was careering toward a precipice, even though the underlying problem pushing me there wasn't always clear. I just thought I was a fortunate young man, blessed to do well in school, have friends, and still engage in so many exciting outside interests. In fact, others used the word *prodigy* to describe my ability to accomplish things I set my mind to. Indeed, at age six, I ran my own little business selling autographed baseball cards. It was really more of a hobby than a moneymaker. My dad set up a table at card shows so I could learn how to interact with adults. My young obsession with player signatures turned out to be a wonderful activity that my dad and I could pursue on my weekend visits with him.

As I grew, I expanded my celebrity targets to include actors, actresses, music stars, political figures, and other prominent leaders. By age 14, I was so persistent and skilled at talking to adults that I had become an old hand at autograph collecting. Besides staking out potential hot spots in New York City, my dad and I would fly between Los Angeles and Washington, D.C., to find any celebrity we recognized as notable. Madonna, Michael Jackson, Brad Pitt, Frank Sinatra, Audrey Hepburn, Patrick Swayze, Steven Spielberg, the Rolling Stones—they all signed. Even Margaret Thatcher, Yasser Arafat, and the Dalai Lama put pen to paper.

I was so determined to get then-President Bill Clinton's autograph that my dad and I waited outside the White House for five hours, hoping he'd come out for a jog. Imagine my excitement when a group of astronauts dressed in jogging gear finally arrived and announced to the guard that they were there to run with the President. Imagine my disappointment when, a few minutes later, they all left in a motorcade. Before I knew it, I was racing after the vehicles on foot as they sped through the city, sailing through each traffic light. We went miles before the cars stopped. I made a final mad dash to get to the President, but the Secret Service shooed me away.

I thought the episode was over, but the television networks caught me on tape flying down the streets, tailing the motorcade. CNN and Headline News even featured me as their lead story that day. When President Clinton heard of my tenacity, he had his office invite our family to the White House. I not only got to shake the President's hand and tour the Oval Office, but I also now have a great picture of us together for my album. Alas, no autograph, however. No "William Jefferson Clinton" adorns my collection, despite my extraordinary efforts.

Even without his "John Hancock," I had amassed more than 1,000 signatures, enough to attract newspaper, radio, and television interest. What could be next? A book, naturally. I tried the big publishers, but when my efforts fell short, my dad and I self-published *Okay, Dad, You Can Take the Picture: A Young Man's Quest for Autographs of the Famous.* My story was featured on more than 300 radio stations, as well as in the *New York Post* and the *Daily News,* and on *Entertainment Tonight.*

My prediagnosis energy (manic or otherwise) was taking me far. I had been doing things that others my age wouldn't think of accomplishing. I was certain that if I could keep this up, I was destined to become a major author or possibly have my own television show. My opinions of myself were that high. I wasn't completely off the mark, since I had already established some credentials. I was hosting a public-access cable-television show, for which I interviewed notable people at charity events, premieres, and parties around New York City.

Through all of the drama, I was still leading a safe and relatively quiet life with my mom and stepfather in Marlboro, New Jersey: street hockey, birthday parties, bar mitzvahs. When I wasn't chasing autographs, I did ordinary kid stuff. People accepted me even though I was precocious and annoying, especially about my autograph adventures. My mother was already concerned enough about my sometimes off-putting behavior that she had me in therapy. I was working on being a kinder, humbler, and less-irritating Blake.

I looked forward to using my new skills when, because of my stepfather's job, we moved to Dix Hills, Long Island. It would be a fresh start. Unfortunately, it didn't work out quite that way. I had problems from the minute I started school. I had no friends. I was a weirdo to the other children. I managed to roil five or six bullies each day on the bus. They were always aiming for a fight, and I was their target. They'd kick, punch, and verbally abuse me. Even though they picked on me mercilessly, I never fought back. It wasn't in my being. But it was the final straw.

Finally, a Diagnosis

My growing isolation as a new kid on the block was one factor in that perfect storm of factors that finally brought everything to a head. I'm certain that the residual trauma from the past abduction plus the immense pressure of hyperachieving to mask my insecurities culminated in the stabbing pain that jolted through my skull at age 15. It was the defining moment that led to my diagnosis.

The pain was no ordinary symptom of bipolar disorder, even though some patients complain of physical ailments like headaches in addition to their mental disturbances. Still, my intense conviction that I was dying in the face of no evidence certainly fit the diagnostic criteria. I was definitely delusional. The throbbing was so intense, however, that I actually believed my brain was bleeding. I spit on my hand and raised it to my head to look for the blood. I couldn't think or function. My heart raced as I begged my mom to take me to the hospital. I was certain I was dying. She called our primary-care physician, who had a sort of "take two aspirin and call me in the morning" attitude. He told her to give me part of a sleeping pill to calm me down.

I was undeterred, however. After hours of hearing me yell about the pain, my mom and stepdad finally hauled me to the emergency room at a hospital in Manhasset, New York. The doctors could find nothing physically wrong. But there were enough red flags for two psychiatrists to order me to be admitted to the psychiatric unit for a complete evaluation. They were alarmed by my unwavering belief that I was about to die. I was also giving them an earful about my "professional" commitments. I told them how I was chasing after celebrities for their autographs and promoting a book on the same topic by contacting television stations. I'm sure my intensity and rapid-fire delivery also gave the doctors pause. Were these activities real or just the rambling delusions of a teenager with some kind of mental problem? They obviously decided they had to find out. (Oddly enough, my concerns were very real!)

I still remember being walked into that locked psychiatric unit. My mother cried at the thought of her 15-year-old son staying alone in such a place. When the door shut, with my family on the outside and me on the inside, I knew my life was about to change forever. It took several weeks, but I finally had a diagnosis of bipolar disorder. I now faced a mental illness accompanied by the traumatic memories of my past—and maybe even partly caused by them.

Setbacks Ahead

Even though I walked out of that hospital after 30 days with a diagnosis and medication, I was hardly on the road to real recovery. It was the first of five hospitalizations. Yes, I said *five*. I had a very difficult time accepting that I was bipolar. Here I was, a 15-year-old with the stigma of a mental disease. I fought it. I was angry, confused, and sad. I went back to collecting my autographs and promoting my book, while attending a special high school for students with similar problems.

Yet over the next two years, I experienced more and more startling episodes. I was convinced, for instance, that I could fly without wings. I was so certain of this possibility that I spent days and nights in the New York Public Library researching it. My thesis as to how this would work took normal male-adolescent fantasizing to new heights. It went like this: I'd build enough arm strength to provide the lift and then count on the charge from my ejaculation to boost and carry me into flight. More specifically, once my penis was inserted into my anus, my ejaculate would provide the "blast" that I needed to take off as I flapped my "wings." *How bizarre is that?* It was not only physiologically impossible, but also limiting, since it could only work for men! Yet in my mind, it had real possibilities. My parents were terrified that I might actually test it. (My invention got me admitted to a psychiatric facility!)

I had other, less peculiar (but no less jarring) episodes. One time I thought my computer had been infiltrated by foreign espionage agents. I was so convincing that the CompUSA store manager gave me free disks to back up my files before the spies could do any harm. Another time, I stayed at Kinko's for 48 hours trying to launch my own magazine. I even created covers with real pictures of me meeting the likes of O. J. Simpson and Tom Cruise, and a doctored one of Pope John Paul II and me. When my dad tried to get me to come home, I fought with him until the two of us took chase through the streets of Manhattan. I darted up and down subway stairs until my dad corralled me. I was convinced that the two female officers he snagged to take me to the hospital were just actresses playing a part in a reality show we were all filming, with me as the star!

I was a wreck. That was just one of several escapades that landed me in a psychiatric facility. I even did "time" in New York's celebrated Bellevue Hospital, a truly creepy place for both the criminally insane and other, less dangerous patients like me. I was delusional at first. I even thought many of the residents were celebrities. The fat guy with the beard was really John Candy, and the thin, red-haired beauty was Julia Roberts in the flesh, no less. Of course, both of them were figments of my delusions, but I was convinced these celebrities were my fellow patients.

My doctors readjusted my meds again. After 30 days, I was out, a little calmer but certainly not healed. Hospitalizations became an all-too-familiar part of my teenage years. My mother and I thought the treatments would never work. The doctors couldn't seem to identify the right drug combination. I would calm down, but within days my manic episodes were back.

It seemed as if my life were over. Adding insult to my already-injured self-esteem, one bipolar "expert," whose advice my mother sought, said I would never finish high school, go to college, get married, have children, or live outside a group home. That was my future. Thankfully, my mother thought differently. She had lost me for ten months to that non-custodial parental abduction; she wasn't about to lose me for the rest of her life. I credit her persistence with finding me the right physician and treatment combination. I had a ways to go to pick up the pieces and make something of a shattered young life.

Change in the Wind

My life changed when my mother and I met Dr. Amy Koreen, a Long Island psychiatrist who not only understood bipolar disorder, but also had a great command of *psychopharmacology,* or the medications to treat mental illness. She was confident that I could overcome my symptoms, and encouraged us not to give up. To control my manic episodes, Dr. Amy took me off the lithium I had been on and put me on two other drugs, a mood stabilizer or anticonvulsant called Depakote and an atypical antipsychotic called Zyprexa. Within a few weeks, my mood swings and hallucinations had calmed down precipitously. Once my doctor found the proper drug combination, I became rational and balanced.

I now had clarity about how close I really had come to losing my chance at a normal life. I finally accepted that without continued treatment, I would quickly revert to my old ways. I'd be destined for a hospital or group home. I knew my life had to change. I wasn't all that religious back then, despite my Jewish upbringing, but I prayed hard to God to give me a second chance. He did! There was one catch, however. My long-term sanity was, for all practical purposes, now up to me!

Over the next decade, I proved to be up to the task. As soon as I was ready, I went back to high school, this time to a special school for children with mental illness so that I could adapt at my own pace. I did well, eventually graduating and starting college at the C. W. Post Campus of Long Island University. I started making new friends and rebuilding my confidence. I realized that as long as I remained stable, I could pursue any goal in my bag of interests.

I was also laying the groundwork for the future I'm enjoying today. I had gone through and learned so much in dealing with my illness that I decided to dedicate my life to helping others do the same. I would be inspired by other events, too. I happened to be in Manhattan at my dad's house when the Twin Towers came down on 9/11. The tragedy reinforced my resolve to do good works in the world.

When my mother, who had been at my side through every good and bad thing, decided to get her master's degree in social work from Adelphi University, it was natural for me to join her. Together, we not only met that challenge, but also opened a joint private practice after graduation. In the years since then, I've had many other positive experiences, including making various professional changes, marrying the love of my life, and starting a family.

I believed then, as I do now, that bipolar was a blessing. Just as God gave me this challenge to overcome, He gave me a purpose, first as a therapist and now as a life coach working with bipolar clients. Every time I can share with people that I *really do* understand their fears and *really do* know that they can do well, I'm confident that I'm in the right place. I see the trust in their eyes from just knowing that, like them, I've had a tempest in my head. I've been there, too!

Bipolar: A Disease of Choices

I'm successful thus far in beating bipolar because I realize the importance of making choices with my illness. No matter what your ultimate diagnosis is, you won't be able to pop a pill and declare yourself well. You'll have to be selective in how you live your life. That's just how healing works with this illness! You'll likely come to many crossroads as you learn about, accept, and address the limitations and possibilities inherent in being bipolar. I did. No one can force you to take one path over another. But if you're looking for a healthy resolution, your choices should be clear, and they are *yours* to make. In the journey from pain to emotional stability, you'll be called upon to:

— **Accept or reject your illness.** Your doctor can give you a diagnosis and tell you all about bipolar disorder, but you're the one who has to acknowledge that you have it. Many people aren't brave enough or invested enough to take on the harmful forces in their lives, much less confront a mental illness. Some of us succumb to the depression, addictions, or even suicide linked to bipolar disorder. If *you* ignore this illness, you're bound to fail, too. By not recognizing your condition, you can't get the correct treatment. By failing to stick with therapy, you'll likely relapse. But if you accept the hand you've been dealt, you'll show amazing courage. I haven't met you personally, but let me congratulate you already. You are a warrior for facing your challenges. Just know that you have the abilities and potential to own and improve your mental and physical health.

— **Accept or reject the work that comes with bipolar disorder.** Life is not a walk in the park for anyone, but if you have a mental illness, you face challenges that often feel insurmountable and unfair. I've met many bipolar individuals who have had difficulties finishing school or holding down jobs. They've watched powerful medications zap their energy. And they've detoured through psychiatric hospitals, not once but numerous times. Yet they've also overcome numerous setbacks and indignities, because they tackled the fallout of their disease. Many of these individuals lead phenomenal lives today. They work. They make a difference in their communities. They successfully demonstrate that people with mental illnesses have great potential, if they're willing to work at it.

— **Accept or reject that you likely will need medication over a lifetime.** The drugs to help you tame your mania and lift your depression are plentiful and effective. Yet they only work if you accept that you must take them, that you'll have to work at finding the right combination, and that you must stick with the regimen. Mood stabilizers, anticonvulsants, antipsychotics, and antidepressants won't work effectively if you chronically miss your schedule or go off them because you're "feeling fine."

— **Accept or reject that you'll need therapy and peer support.** We share many trials as bipolar individuals, but isolation may be the most profound among them. Feeling alone is a universal experience for people with any mental illness, particularly this one. Not surprisingly, there are many reasons for it. Perhaps you're so embarrassed about your mood swings and the past damage linked to your illness that you don't reach out to others. Or maybe you have too many bottled-up feelings stemming from other personal baggage to connect easily. Whatever the driving force, working with a mental health professional will help you sort out your issues and learn to connect with people. Moreover, by joining a peer group, you'll have a place to talk about your struggles and become socially savvy.

— **Accept or reject that your family's participation and role in your life and illness might have to be modified to suit your healing.** Many of us with bipolar disorder rely on our parents and siblings for emotional support. It's wonderful when you've been able to nurture strong bonds with family members. But sometimes it's not clear what roles the people biologically closest to you can or should actually play. Since your illness and other family dynamics or history can be a source of stress and strain, you'll need to decide if these people are the kind of supporters you can count on for the long haul. If so, how can you have an honest, open relationship? If not, how can you create a different type of support system? You'll need answers to those questions to live in a connected way.

— Accept or reject that you have to change aspects of your life-style. The reality of your illness and the medications your doctor prescribes to treat it is that neither mixes well with illicit drugs and alcohol. Drinking and substance abuse can cloud your thinking and shortchange your decision making. They can be lethal when combined with your meds, especially if your moods are not regulated yet. Even if you'd like a drink now and then, you need to check with your doctor. Along with diet, exercise, and plenty of sleep, abstaining or moderation is part of living healthy with a mental illness.

— Accept or reject that bipolar isn't an end; it's a beginning. The choice is yours. The knee-jerk reaction to a mental illness is often to cower or run, especially if you think there's nothing to be gained in fighting. But this is a chance to examine your life, shake off what's not working, and become a better version of yourself! I believe the struggles in our lives are put here solely to teach us lessons and help us grow. When we experience pain, we have a chance to rise to the occasion. I'm confident that you have the courage to take on anything. No matter how hard life has been in the past, I know you're strong enough to deal with the challenges in the future. The payoff? A life filled with what I call the four affirming *H*'s: *hope, health, happiness,* and *healing!*

One Final Note

I live every day with the fact that I have a chronic illness. As healthy as I am, I never completely forget that my symptoms could return. Of course, as long as I take my medications, I have a very good chance of staying balanced, even if my drugs and dosages may change at some point. But I also pay particular attention to my behavior. If I'm at a party and someone is downing ten shots on a dare, I know I can only look on. If my colleague needs someone to stay up all night for a project, I have to take a pass. Others may think that I'm shirking my professional duties, but I honestly need my sleep. (And I don't mean for beauty!)

Whatever constraints I experience today, however, I know that wellness is much preferable to being out of control. When I look back on my life prior to the diagnosis, I can see my insecurities and mood swings clearly. I turned away friends and alienated others. Even in the face of my young "successes," things were pretty difficult, especially for those who loved me. I never want to return to that place.

Each of us has a unique history and journey. We're all at different places in our lives. But I can imagine what you're facing based on my own experience in dealing with bipolar disorder and helping others address this condition. I believe in my heart and gut that you're up to the task of mastering your illness. I trust that you're a wonderful human being who deserves to experience the very best in life. The advice in *Beating Bipolar* can help you do just that!

● ● ●

CHAPTER TWO

THE POWER OF A DIAGNOSIS

HEARING OFFICIALLY THAT you have bipolar disorder can be overwhelming. It's frightening to know that you're suffering from a mental illness, let alone to learn that you'll have to tend it for the rest of your life. That is, of course, unless someone finds a cure. It's like staring into the abyss. You don't know if you should stick with the verdict or get a second opinion.

Rest assured, though. Having an official diagnosis for your symptoms really is a good thing. Yes, I said, a good thing! You'll finally have a name for your erratic behavior and a game plan to deal with it. Also, bipolar can be progressive. If not monitored and treated, the less serious bipolar II, for instance, can turn into the more serious bipolar I, and untreated bipolar I just goes from bad to worse. (We'll explore the differences in depth later in this chapter.) By getting diagnosed early, however, you can prevent one type from morphing into the other or either type from just going downhill.

Physicians have come a long way in their understanding of this disease and its manic-depressive episodes. In the not-so-distant past, bipolar was often just lumped with other psychotic disorders such as schizophrenia, a different, albeit serious, cognitive condition marked by incoherent speech, delusions, and hallucinations. But because physicians have a better grasp of mental illnesses now than ever before, it's well within their reach to diagnose bipolar correctly, including the specific type.

Don't get me wrong. Doctors sometimes miss symptoms as part of a larger problem. People can suffer for years before they're properly diagnosed and treated, sometimes because they either don't find the right clinician or they ignore the signs in front of them. Others *hear* the words *bipolar disorder,* but it takes much longer to adjust to the reality of them.

What's in a Name?

In writing this book, I use both *bipolar disorder* and *bipolar* in reference to our shared mental illness. You may wonder what the terms actually mean, however. *Bipolar disorder* reflects the dual nature of what you're experiencing. "Bi" and "polar" refer to the two distinct phases of this illness: the "up," or manic, episodes and the "down," or depressive, episodes. That's different from *major depressive disorder,* which, in medical speak, is described as *monopolar* or *unipolar,* since sufferers experience only one side of the spectrum, the depression. They don't have the elevated moods. Sometimes our condition is called *bipolar affective disorder. Affective* is just another way of recognizing that the predominant characteristic is a major disturbance of moods, thoughts, or behaviors. Whether it's *bipolar disorder* or *bipolar affective disorder,* the results are the same: a lifelong challenge.

I resisted the idea of a chronic mental illness long after I first received my diagnosis. I had been in the midst of a manic episode and was feeling invincible, so the last words I expected or wanted to hear in that psychiatric hospital were "You are sick." At 15, I was frightened about what other children would think. Would I be ostracized for being different? Would a mental illness mean I was tainted or unworthy of friends?

Would I have to live my life alone? These were more than lingering fears. They haunted me. I was constantly worried about the future and embarrassed about my current situation. I was on lithium at first, which made me go to the bathroom frequently and gave me a tremor. I also hated that I had spent time in a psychiatric hospital. In my mind, it was just a loony bin for people who were violent, evil, and a danger to society. I was none of those things! The stigma of this disease was a major reason why I didn't accept my diagnosis initially. That would be like admitting I was "crazy." I wasn't "crazy."

I hadn't learned an important lesson that I now repeat freely to my clients: put aside what society says for the moment. The sooner you are properly diagnosed and accept your condition, the sooner you can actively engage in healing. By taking action now, you can live happily and productively, and be financially secure!

If You Haven't Been Diagnosed

If you don't know why you're exhibiting sadness that's more than the run-of-the-mill blues, or elation too unfettered to be a normal high, you need to be evaluated by someone who is very familiar with bipolar disorder.

Unfortunately, the reality for many of us is that we're diagnosed when we're out of control and hospitalized for our own protection. An emergency can bring any mental illness into quick focus, especially when you're in the care of people who are familiar with it. They've been down this road with other patients, so they're prepared to evaluate what's happening in pretty short order. In my own case, psychiatrists diagnosed me with bipolar I, the most severe form, during my first admission.

But isn't it safer to find out what you're battling when you're not in crisis than to wait until you're in full-blown mania or ready to take your own life? I think so! There are great advantages in digesting the information and making a plan long before catastrophe hits. By taking control of your illness, you can be on the road to wellness and recovery rather than facing an emotional crisis or another mood swing.

Mental health professionals (usually psychiatrists, but often clinical psychologists) who specialize in this condition rely on their experience and training in not only diagnosing your bipolar disorder but also identifying the specific type affecting you. I'm often asked if an internist or family physician can provide an adequate mental health assessment. A general practitioner can certainly give you an initial read on your symptoms and make a referral. But you need a professional who has been trained to read your symptoms and evaluate them against any other possible sources to make an accurate call.

Unfortunately, there's no one test, blood or otherwise, to isolate bipolar. (Wouldn't it be nice if a pinprick or draw could give us answers?) Instead, your doctor will evaluate you by combining experience and skill with observation and a thorough clinical interview. Doctors use various standardized assessment instruments in systematically evaluating symptoms against established criteria for a bipolar diagnosis. The most widely used source in the United States is the American Psychiatric Association's *Diagnostic and Statistical Manual of Mental Disorders* (*DSM-IV-TR*).

Your work-up will rely heavily on the conversation between you and your doctor about your symptoms. You'll want to provide honest answers to the many questions posed to you. Whether you undergo a mental health assessment in a hospital unit, a free clinic, or your psychiatrist's office, the focus will be on your life history, family background, and social or relationship issues. It will include very specific inquiries about the frequency, severity, and length of your mood swings, as well as your experience with anxiety, racing thoughts, and impulsive behavior. You'll be asked about how much your actions are interfering with your daily routine or even leading you to think of suicide. You even may have to chart your highs, lows, sleep patterns, and other factors. Because bipolar has a strong genetic component, your doctor will be interested in any familial history of mental illnesses, especially if either of your parents or any of your siblings are similarly affected. (Fortunately or unfortunately, I was the first in my family.) By the time you're through with the interview, your physician should have a good idea of what's causing your erratic behavior.

Other Conditions

A thorough diagnostic evaluation will allow your doctor to rule out secondary health issues that may coexist with your manic depression. Bipolar disorder is a complicated illness for any number of reasons, not the least of which is that it often involves other issues. Numerous studies have shown a link between this mental illness and various anxiety disorders: obsessive-compulsive disorder (OCD), panic disorder, phobic disorder, social anxiety disorder, and post-traumatic stress disorder (PTSD). Also, the symptoms of ADHD or attention deficit/hyperactivity disorder overlap with bipolar, making it difficult to differentiate the two conditions. (I've had other struggles to address besides my bipolar, but none of the above was among them.)

Your doctor will also screen for drug or alcohol problems. Substance abuse is a major health hazard that can trigger symptoms similar to those of mania or depression. It's also a frequent dueling health issue with bipolar disorder and other mental illnesses, which can complicate recovery. Unless you actively manage the problem, your bipolar will be infinitely more difficult to address.

Whatever you're asked, it's critical that you're open with your answers and willing to let others offer their observations concerning your erratic behavior. Since your doctor can glean insight from those around you, it's a good idea to give him or her permission to query those closest to you. They likely see you in a different, objective light. Also, since your bipolar can change throughout your lifetime, share everything that you're experiencing at the moment. Your treatment won't be effective unless it's keyed to your current situation. So speak up. Your recovery depends on it!

Blood Tests

Although a bipolar diagnosis is usually made from a psychological evaluation, your doctor may order blood and other laboratory tests to assess your general health or rule out other underlying health issues. The symptoms are often associated with serious infections or chronic diseases, such as diabetes, lupus, hyperthyroidism or hypothyroidism (overactive or underactive thyroid), kidney failure, HIV, and even syphilis. They also may be triggered by certain drugs, such as steroid medications that are taken for inflammatory disease such as rheumatoid arthritis, ulcerative colitis, asthma, allergies, or psoriasis. Don't be surprised if your doctor calls for blood studies to rule out other issues or to see if certain systems are working properly.

High-Tech Tests

Diagnosing bipolar disorder is a relatively low-tech rather than high-tech endeavor. Sophisticated imaging tests such as an MRI (magnetic resonance imaging) or CT (computerized tomography) scan aren't generally used to diagnose bipolar disorder, even though studies continue to explore their value. Your doctor, however, may order such specialized tests to establish certain neurological baselines, rule out other underlying medical issues, or prep you for specific treatments. He or she may want to exclude a possible brain tumor, for instance. You also may undergo an electroencephalogram (EEG), a painless test that measures your brain's electrical activity. Besides excluding seizure disorders or tumors, EEGs are used for other purposes, such as preparation for ECT (electroconvulsive therapy), a therapy often used to calm mood swings when medications are not helping. In a similar pretreatment vein, you may undergo an EKG (electrocardiogram) to measure cardioelectrical performance. Since certain medications can affect your heart, your doctor may want a baseline and perhaps follow-ups.

Tracking a Mental Illness
. . . .

If you have bipolar, you're actually part of history. This disorder has been around since the beginning of recorded time, with religious and mythological texts from many cultures referencing the distinct symptoms.

Ancient Roman and Greek physicians—most notably Hippocrates, the father of Western medicine—first coined the terms *melancholia* and *mania* to describe the states we recognize today as depression and abnormal euphoria. Their designations reflected a prevailing medical theory (called the *humoral theory*) of the day. That is, a mix of four fluids—*black bile, yellow* or *red bile, blood,* and *phlegm*—governed a person's constitution. Balance meant health, while imbalance triggered disease. More specifically, *melancholia* was the result of an excess of black bile. *Mania* was an excess of yellow bile. The great thinkers of the day also tied specific organs to the process. Hippocrates believed that melancholia involved an underlying biological disturbance in the brain, while the great Greek philosopher Aristotle saw it as involving the heart.

Even though there were hints over time that melancholia and mania might be connected, these patterns weren't viewed as diverse expressions of the same illness. They were largely considered separate entities, yet debilitating just the same. During the next centuries, philosophers and scholars grappled with the intersection of body, mind, and emotions, particularly in terms of strange moods.

It wasn't until the middle to late 1800s that the modern concept of *manic depression* as a single disease was born. Nineteenth-century thinkers laid the groundwork, led by two French physicians, Jules Baillarger and Jean-Pierre Falret. With their respective *folie à double* and *folie circulaire,* they independently formulated the idea that one illness indeed could cause two distinct mood stages. Both men were on to something, but it was left to German psychiatrist Emil Kraepelin to take the idea to the next logical stage.

He segregated psychotic disorders such as *dementia praecox,* or "premature madness," now referred to as *schizophrenia,* from melancholy. In so doing, he was not only separating thought or cognitive problems from emotional or affective issues, but also suggesting the term *manic depressive* for those in the latter category. The term wasn't just a synonym for what we know today as "bipolar disorder," however. Kraepelin swept all depressive episodes into the same general category, whether they were recurrent events of what we now call "clinical depression" or part of a more insidious chronic depression-into-mania cycle.

Yet he provided physicians with a diagnostic classification system and other nuanced information—such as the roles of psychological and social variables along with biological vulnerabilities in triggering each episode—so that they could start navigating the terrain.

Needless to say, doctors and scientists craved more information about the differences than what Kraepelin offered in his 1913 textbook. By the early 1950s, other psychiatrists, most notably Karl Leonhard, had generated enough new evidence to bridge some of the gaps. Leonhard pioneered a classification system that validated family history as an important criterion in addition to clinical markers in identifying this mental illness. Patients with bipolar not only suffered symptoms at two ends, or "poles," of the emotional spectrum (mania and depression), but also had a higher incidence of mania in their families than did *unipolar* patients, or those who suffered major depressive disorder alone.

It took another 30 years before *bipolar disorder* made it into the *Diagnostic and Statistical Manual of Mental Disorders,* the bible of psychiatric classifications. But its presence there and in other respected directories confirms just how far physicians have come in defining and understanding this disorder. Of course, there's much more to the story and much more to learn about the mechanisms driving this mental illness. Yet knowing that the pattern of symptoms confirms a real, definable illness gives patients like us the chance for real treatment and real success.

. . . .

Breaking Down Bipolar

Scientists have yet to piece together the entire bipolar puzzle, but they know that there are distinct variants or types of this illness that have a direct bearing on the severity of your episodes and your ultimate treatment. In diagnosing your condition, your doctor will focus on the following possibilities:

— **Bipolar I.** The most debilitating end of the spectrum, bipolar I needs lifelong treatment because of the severity and frequency of the episodes. Each manic, depressive, or mixed bout (mania and depression combined) lasts at least seven days and can be so severe that it disrupts every corner and function of your life. It can also lead to immediate hospitalization. Individuals with undiagnosed or untreated bipolar I are at risk for psychotic breaks with reality. If you hear voices, have paranoid thoughts, or show signs of other disruptive thinking, you need emergency care. The key to bipolar I is that it produces major, even dangerous, changes to your normal behavior that require ongoing treatment to right the ship.

Treatment focus: For mania, your doctor will recommend medication to calm your brain, plus lifestyle changes (modifying your sleep routine and adding activities such as relaxation techniques) to slow your pace. For depression, he or she will suggest tracking your moods and incorporating activities to lift them. You'll also be strongly urged to meet with a therapist to address the underlying psychological issues tangled up with your illness. If you're suicidal, you'll definitely need to be hospitalized.

— **Bipolar II.** Although individuals diagnosed with bipolar II don't experience full-blown mania or mixed manic and depressive episodes, they still shift between depression and *hypomania,* a less intense, albeit still significant, version of a manic state. You can have persistent elevated, energized moods and changes in your ability to function. Yet you likely can carry on with your normal daily routine.

That's not to say that people might not sense that there's a problem. You may have racing thoughts or be easily distracted or agitated with hypomania. But the level at which all of this occurs is different from that of a full-blown manic attack. For instance, if you're in hypomania, you might chat incessantly at a party. If you're in full-blown mania, you might grab the microphone, climb on a table, or even strip!

Although bipolar I individuals can experience hypomania, too, bipolar II individuals don't have the kind of psychoses or delusional symptoms that land them in the hospital. If left unchecked, however, the condition can progress to the more serious stage.

Sometimes it's difficult to spot bipolar II during hypomania, because individuals just seem productive and happy. It's during depressive episodes, which usually last longer than hypomania, that someone notices a problem since the person simply can't get off the dime.

Treatment focus: For hypomania, the emphasis is on calming your mind with medication plus meditation, relaxation, and exercise. You may also be encouraged to de-stress by journaling about your symptoms and feelings, and improving your sleep routine. Since bipolar II depression can be as crippling as that of bipolar I, you'll need to treat it in the same aggressive way so that you don't entertain suicidal thoughts or actions.

— **Cyclothymia.** The key word in describing this type of bipolar disorder is *mild.* Individuals diagnosed with cyclothymia experience shifting episodes of hypomania and depression over at least two years. Although the episodes may even be disruptive, the highs and lows associated with them aren't severe enough to merit designation as "major." If you're diagnosed with cyclothymia, you may have some problems functioning but nothing close to those experienced by individuals with bipolar II, let alone bipolar I.

Treatment focus: For both mania and depression, the same medication, therapy, and other techniques used for bipolar I and II can be applied very successfully for cyclothymia. The important point to remember is that although this is perhaps a less drastic form of bipolar, it still impacts you.

— **Bipolar disorder not otherwise specified (BP-NOS).** People who are diagnosed with BP-NOS don't meet the criteria of any type of bipolar disorder, even though they exhibit symptoms that are definitely outside their normal behavior and in line with this mental illness. In other words, you may have all of the indicators in your history and behavior, but your doctor can't make the call because your episodes don't last long enough or your symptoms are too few in number. That doesn't mean that your problems aren't real or potentially disruptive, however. You still need to be under a doctor's care. It just means that, for now, you can't put the words *bipolar I, bipolar II,* or *cyclothymia* to them.

Treatment focus: For mania and depression, even though you aren't diagnosed specifically with bipolar disorder, your doctor will draw from the same pool of treatment options in recommending a plan individualized to your unique circumstances. That includes medications to deal with your mania, depression, and any psychoses, combined with therapy, support, and lifestyle changes.

Variations on a Common Theme

Despite your diagnosis, the nature of bipolar is that it manifests in different ways. Like me, you may be most concerned about mania, but then again, your focus might be depression. Or perhaps you have significant trouble with both cycles. You may have singular, brief episodes of your symptoms or repeated episodes of depression, mania, and hypomania.

If those patterns show up concurrently or in rapid succession, you have what's called *mixed bipolar.* You can be agitated and hyperactive at the same time that you're deeply sad and de-energized. I know it's hard to imagine that someone can be ecstatic and miserable at the same time, but the nature of this mental illness is that the symptoms defy predictability.

You may also undergo *rapid-cycling bipolar disorder,* which means that your mood shifts are in such high gear that they're changing at a fast and furious rate. Rapid cycling comes into play when you experience four or more episodes of major depression, mania, hypomania, or mixed symptoms within one year. In extreme cases, it can be within a week, day, or hours.

Whatever your manifestations, mood swings are often interspersed with periods of normal behavior, which can be brief or last for years. If you seem to be in "remission," don't get lulled into thinking that you no longer have a problem. If not treated, your bipolar episodes are bound to increase in frequency and severity. Any delay in getting diagnosed officially can increase your likelihood of encountering all sorts of problems, including a change in your fate.

Bipolar and Adolescents

Learning that your teenager has bipolar disorder can be a frighteningly confusing experience. You may not know (or want to believe) that your child's behavior seems a tad off-kilter. Or you may pick up on the clues, but they don't register as adding up to bipolar disorder unless, of course, it's already in the family. Then you might recognize the symptoms. As I can attest, finding bipolar disorder in this age group is not so rare, since more than half of all cases of this mental illness surface between ages 15 and 25.[1] (Although it's much less common in younger children, when the condition occurs in these patients, it's referred to as *early-onset bipolar disorder*.)

Despite the prevalence, pinning down the diagnosis in teens is difficult, if not controversial, especially since many of the symptoms mimic mental health mood problems common in young people, such as ADHD and oppositional defiant disorder (ODD). Adolescents also don't exhibit their mania or depression in the same distinct ways that adults exhibit their symptoms. Instead the signs often resemble the typical ups and downs and rebellious behavior of a teenager: irritability and temper tantrums; erratic shifts in mood, energy levels, and behavior; recklessness; and aggression. Also, while adults tend to have clear-cut periods of depression and mania lasting for weeks, months, or even longer, young people frequently experience daily occurrences of both manifestations, sometimes even with simultaneous hits. These episodes also may have been surfacing for months, if not years.

Because of those factors, doctors don't always agree on the best way to diagnose adolescents. The debate centers on using the same *DSM-*

IV-TR criteria used successfully for adults. Although some experts are satisfied with the standards, others think the one-size-fits-all approach doesn't go far enough to account for the nuanced differences that young people experience with this mental illness. It doesn't do enough to separate bipolar disorder from other conditions that produce similar symptoms, particularly in young people.

So how do physicians hit the diagnostic nail squarely on the head, especially since the teen experience might not be a tidy fit for *DSM* criteria? Some experts suggest that by targeting behaviors unique to bipolar disorder but largely uncommon with similar illnesses, doctors can accurately pinpoint this condition. For instance, since one of the biggest challenges is to differentiate mania from ADHD, the best way to isolate bipolar disorder is to zero in on irritability in addition to other core bipolar symptoms: unexplained euphoria, grandiose behavior, racing thoughts, risky activities, decreased sleep, and even hallucinations.

What's the Message for You as a Parent?

If your child seems to be infectiously happy when there's no reason to be intensely giddy or acts as if the normal rules of decorum don't apply to him or her, don't pass it off as just bad or weird teenage behavior. If your child's emotions are swinging from intense silliness and abnormal highs to angry outbursts or gloomy tear-filled lows within a day or even hours, you need to pay close attention. Likewise, if your teen is flitting from one thought or activity to another, or needs appreciably more or less shut-eye than normal, you need to contact your pediatrician. (Clearly if your child is delusional, you're in emergency territory. Remember my bleeding brain? My bipolar was on full display!)

Although your child's doctor can give you general feedback as to what he or she observes, you'll likely need and want a referral to a mental health professional who is skilled in diagnosing and dealing with adolescent bipolar disorder. Whether you start with a psychotherapist or psychiatrist, it's important early on to involve a specialist who knows how this mental illness manifests in young people, given that it's markedly different than it is in adults. In making a definitive diagnosis, a professional will know what to look for and ask about in terms of each potential symptom. (Family history of the disorder or other mental illnesses will be especially important, for instance, since genetics can be a key indicator.)

Whether your child meets with a therapist initially or as part of treatment, he or she likely will need counseling to deal with many issues, not the least of which is how to cope with the diagnosis and learn everything possible about the disease. Beyond that, the emotional land mines with this mental illness can be significant. You and your child will need new skills to face a broad range of concerns, from grappling with a lifelong illness to tackling learning issues and problems with social interactions or family relationships.

If your doctor suggests family therapy and group support, I strongly suggest that you take this advice. You need all hands on deck, including those of your child's teachers and school counselors. It's important to let any essential person know that a chronic mental illness may affect your son or daughter's performance. You may even want feedback during diagnosis if you think that someone else can offer relevant insight as to what he or she sees in class.

As to medications, even though your child is just a child, he or she likely will have to be medicated. Bipolar disorder in adolescents and children is an emerging field, so very little research exists as to the long-term effectiveness or even safety of medications in younger people. Not all drugs used in treating bipolar disorder are FDA-approved for teens. (None are approved for children under age 10.) The ones that are considered safe and effective in younger patients have only been studied in the short term, meaning that scientists know how they'll behave in the immediate future but don't know the impact or side effects in the long term. (Lithium and several atypical antipsychotics, for instance, have been FDA-approved for ages 10 to 17, depending on the drug, while anticonvulsants have not been approved for treating bipolar youth.)

Whatever your child requires, the doctor will take various factors into consideration, including symptoms and potential drug side effects. It's important that you work with a physician who not only understands how to manage youth bipolar disorder but also has a thorough grasp of the limited scientific data available about the long-term effects of each drug in younger people. Because these medications can cause side effects, particularly marked weight gain, you want a mental health professional who can help you assess the pros and cons of drug therapy, in light of the dangers of this mental illness. That person should also be capable of adjusting your child's therapy as necessary.

• •

The sooner you get help for your son or daughter, the better the chance for a good outcome. In my own case, my behavior had escalated to such frightening levels that I had to be hospitalized to finally figure out what was what. If my parents had been familiar with the term *bipolar disorder* and known what it meant, I'm confident they would have been much more aggressive than they were initially in getting me help. Hindsight is always 20/20, but I likely would have struggled less and maybe even enjoyed my teen years more. Just being a teenager means that facing myriad problems—peer pressure, bullying, academic overload, and the anxiety that comes with socializing and developing a self-image. When you throw in signs of a mental illness, the ante for suffering goes up exponentially. As painful as it is to think that your child has bipolar disorder, it's worse to think of what might occur if it's not diagnosed and treated.

Keeping Your Body Tuned!

In diagnosing your bipolar, your doctor will likely call for or do a physical examination. As I said, there are no biological tests to confirm this condition, but your physician will want to know the general state of your health as well as rule out any other issues.

That shouldn't be the last time you see your physician, however. When you have a mental illness, it's easy to concentrate only on the *mental* part of your recovery. Certainly, there are enough challenges related to bipolar disorder to keep you focused and engaged. Yet you need to pay attention to your *physical* well-being, too. You can't heal completely unless your body is in tip-top shape or you're at least working in that direction. You're better positioned to mend your soul, mind, and heart when you improve your lifestyle, see your physician regularly, and work on your overall health.

I know that sometimes it's difficult to find the time, especially if you have a demanding job or you're taking care of a family. Many of us put the needs of others ahead of our own, especially if we're designated caretakers. But this is precisely when you need to carve out time for your own healthy to-do list. No matter where you are in your bipolar journey—whether you are getting a diagnosis or are well into treatment—you want your body on your side.

After graduate school I worked for a nonprofit agency, helping homeless New Yorkers find shelter, clothing, meals, and sometimes even therapy. It was hard seeing these men and women suffer, especially during the blistering cold winters. I was so overwhelmed and stressed by the nature of the job that I started bingeing on high-fat foods. I had reached my highest weight in two years when my supervisor announced a Weight Watchers group for the office. It was a godsend. I learned not only healthy strategies for taking off the pounds, but also the importance of taking "me" time each day. I instituted a healthier diet, including fruit smoothies, and took vitamins. I started hiking and going for long walks. I even joined a pickup basketball game on occasion. I grew stronger physically at the same time that I was getting a psychological workout. I was letting out my emotions while burning calories.

I still struggle to maintain my weight, but today I also try to take better care of myself. I've even persuaded my wife, Jen, to carve out time from her busy schedule as a full-time physician's assistant. Her workdays helping people with urological conditions are demanding and often long. Then she comes home to tend to our daughter, Tyler, and me. We love the time we spend together, but for Jen to be her own best friend, she takes time for herself. She runs every morning, hikes on occasion, and gets a back massage now and then. Both of us are doing things to improve our outlook and get a healthier handle on life. You need to do the same!

"Doctor, Just a Few Questions, Please"

Once you've heard the diagnosis, your next goal is to start working with your physician on a game plan. You'll likely have many questions about the future, especially the practical implications of starting treatment and making changes in your life. Don't expect to take in everything at once; you can't possibly tackle all the nuances in one fell swoop. In writing *Beating Bipolar*, I've just touched on the major points that have facilitated my recovery and helped my clients. Your provider will design the best long-term plan for you. But let me suggest a few questions that might bear asking up front.

— **"Why me, doctor?"** Your physician may or may not have the answer to this question. You'll probably discuss your family background and personal history in searching for any clues as to why these mood swings are happening to *you*. Your provider may point to genetics as a possibility or even a difference in the way your brain functions. But he or she also may have little more insight to offer since we still don't know everything there is to know about bipolar disorder. If you have any doubts about the diagnosis or fears concerning what the future holds, don't be afraid to voice them. You wouldn't be the first person to think that your symptoms are just related to fatigue and stress, or fear that you're bound for a psychiatric hospital or group home. Doubts are par for the course. What you need, however, is a realistic evaluation from your mental health professional about where you're headed. It's very difficult to recover if you don't accept that bipolar is real, and undergo proper treatment. It's very doable if you're resigned to the fact of your illness and resolved to beat it. You can live happily and fulfilled.

— **"Are you available to treat me?"** Chances are that if you haven't already, you'll receive your diagnosis from a psychiatrist or clinical psychologist, mental health professionals usually tasked with identifying bipolar disorder. But what will be this person's role in your future treatment? Will you see the doctor for medications *and* psychotherapy? Or must you be referred? If, by chance, the person who diagnoses you isn't available for follow-through, you need to add others to your care team.

— **"What will my treatment entail?"** You want to be very specific with your mental health professional in determining the best treatment plan for you. If you're going to be on medication, get the skinny from your psychiatrist about what each drug is for, how it works, and why you need it. You might ask how other patients with your symptoms have fared on the same medication. Also, how does your doctor anticipate isolating a stabilizing dosage for you? Does he or she start low and increase at intervals, or start high and decrease as you go forward? Whatever the choice, why so? If you'll be on a combination of drugs or if you take other medications, you definitely want to ask about potential interactions. If you're seeing a therapist, make sure you understand how many times a week or month the two of you will be meeting and just what results he or she anticipates from those sessions.

— **"What changes do I have to make in my personal life to accommodate my illness?"** Beating bipolar is not just a matter of taking pills and attending therapy sessions. Unless you're totally committed to retooling other aspects of your life, you won't realize the value added to your formal treatment plan. It's just common sense to exercise, take care with your diet, and get plenty of sleep. If you didn't have a mental illness, these would be important lifestyle choices. But with a chronic condition, they become even more critical, since how you live can affect relapses and healing. Healthy decisions will help stabilize your moods.

— **"How have other patients you've treated done with their bipolar?"** Clearly it's important to know that your psychiatrist or therapist has helped other individuals achieve stability. But you want to hear both the good and the bad. Be blunt in your inquiries: "What usually happens when progress doesn't occur?" "What do you think my chances are of controlling this illness?" If your doctor says he or she has never met anyone with bipolar who's okay, then move on. You need a mental health professional who believes in your complete recovery and offers you hope that life can change for the better with the right treatment plan. Even a whiff of anything less is unacceptable!

One Final Note

Remember that bipolar disorder doesn't get better by itself. Without a proper diagnosis, you can't get proper treatment. Without proper treatment, your prognosis will worsen with each subsequent episode. You are less and less likely to regain complete normal function. A great tragedy with this mental illness is that many people become so used to the mood swings that they don't realize just how much their emotional instability is disrupting their lives and the lives of people around them. Or they actually feed on being euphoric and manically productive. They're addicted to the highs until the next emotional crash leaves them exhausted, depressed, and possibly facing myriad financial, legal, or relationship problems, not to mention poor work or school performance. Undiagnosed and untreated bipolar can wreak havoc of all sorts, including leaving you isolated and lonely. It can make you a pariah at work or school, especially if your actions are frightening others who don't understand what's going on. It can also increase your risk of becoming suicidal.

If diagnosed and managed carefully, however, bipolar disorder doesn't have to be your undoing. You can live a long, fruitful life filled with a treasure trove of great experiences and friends.

●   ●   ●

PART II

TACKLING YOUR ILLNESS

CHAPTER THREE

MEETING THE BIPOLAR CHALLENGE

BIPOLAR DISORDER CAN affect your internal compass in such a way that you can't carry on normal relationships or have ordinary productive days. Unless you keep your symptoms in check, you can look forward to a life of unending challenges, tensions, and far-reaching negative consequences.

How do you control your condition so that it can't wreak havoc in every nook and cranny of your life? The reassuring news is that you can attain and maintain the same normal emotions that nonbipolar people experience instinctively. There may be no panacea for this disorder, but there's a clear path for living a healthy, productive life in the face of everything negative.

Recovery starts when you acknowledge your mental illness, learn as much as you can about it, understand your symptoms and their ramifications, and then do everything in your power to take control. People who live successfully with bipolar disorder understand that they have a chronic illness that won't get better on its own. They accept the fact that there's no cure. And they work every day on making sure that their moods stay within acceptable ranges. Your goal is not to become so manic that you can't function or so depressed that you lose interest in life or hurt yourself. It's to achieve a healthy balance between excitement and sadness. It's to control your illness by controlling your thoughts, behavior, and time.

Although there are many pieces to the treatment puzzle, if you haven't already, you'll likely need to make dramatic changes to your life. What does that mean? Your best shot to beat bipolar is to work with mental health professionals so that you're accurately diagnosed, properly medicated, and effectively dealing with the emotional issues tied to your illness. Once you've created that team, addressing your bipolar will be largely up to you. You'll be structuring your life in such a way that you don't trigger either a manic or depressive episode. Instead you stay on an even keel.

There are many practical steps you can take to help avert both crises. I've spent an entire chapter, for instance, on what I call "life tools": everyday things you can do to alter how you see yourself and operate within the world. To use those tactics effectively, however, you need to understand your illness. Knowledge is power, as they say. By knowing what you're facing, you'll also know the urgency of addressing it.

Calming the Mania

If being manic just meant that you had high energy levels and the drive to reach for and accomplish new goals, it would be a good thing, right? Who wouldn't like being excited and thrilled by life? But the mania linked to bipolar disorder is more than just your average elevated thoughts or feelings. What's different for you is that you actually feel superpower energy and drug-like euphoria. I liken mania to riding a roller coaster. Your heart races, your mind speeds, and your adrenaline pumps as you take the electrifying twists and turns. Fun, yes, but there are limits to the high-speed ups, downs, and hairpin curves of such a thrill ride. It's unhealthy to subject your body to sustained "rocket" forces again, again, and again.

It's equally unhealthy to subject yourself to the hyper-highs of mania. If left unchecked, each episode can do great damage emotionally and even physically. It can cause you to pursue frightening choices that will not end well: risky sex, excessive speeding, picking fights with your boss, or beating up on your parents. Perhaps you recognize these scenarios as your own. Or maybe you're the person who gambles away your family's life savings or spends thousands on one indiscriminate shopping spree.

Whatever your manifestations, if left untreated, they only worsen. They may also lead to dangerous psychotic episodes, or "breaks" with reality. That's when you lose track of the world around you. Although your thoughts, visions, and behaviors seem appropriate to you, they're completely inappropriate and even incoherent to everyone else.

We often associate the characteristic signs of a psychotic break with another serious mental illness, called *schizophrenia.* But bipolar I individuals are prone to similar hallucinations: hearing, seeing, and experiencing things that just aren't there. They also may have beliefs about themselves that simply aren't true. You've heard of *delusions of grandeur?* They can be part of a bipolar psychotic break, too. You're so out of touch with reality that you're parading around the neighborhood dressed in a white sheet because you think you're Jesus Christ. Or you simply feel paranoid, jealous, or persecuted. Whether such delusions occur during a manic or depressive cycle, they can send you into a very dark place.

The most severe case of mania I've ever dealt with professionally involved Gabie, a young woman whose mother brought her to see me because of her destructive behavior. Gabie was smart, pretty, and creatively blessed. During normalcy, she loved pursuing many refined activities: painting, sculpting, dancing, and writing.

Yet when her manic phase kicked in, she was out of control and living dangerously. Gabie went from sensitive to sexually promiscuous, picking up two or three men a night from a local bar for unprotected sex. If that weren't bad enough, during one of many destructive incidents, she caused quite a scene in her parents' backyard, stripping and painting a canvas with her naked body as her mother's friends looked on. The woman had no shame. Her mother tried to control the situation. But my soon-to-be client raged that the devil had made her do it as she smashed vases, kicked in doors, and threw everything out of the refrigerator.

Panicked about what to do, her mother finally called me at the suggestion of a mutual friend. Once I heard the story, I told her that her daughter needed to be hospitalized immediately so that she could be stabilized. Gabie was in the throes of a manic episode that warranted aggressive management. To her mother's credit, she moved quickly to get Gabie admitted and start her recovery. As this young woman illustrated so graphically, unbridled, frenzied mania can hurt your life and the lives of others you touch. Unless you get off the ride or put on some brakes, you either spin out of control or free-fall into depression. Neither is a stable place.

Even though I saw Gabie during her psychiatric stay, she refused further help after being released. Two years later, much to my surprise, she called for an appointment. The tastefully coiffed and immaculately dressed woman who walked into my office barely resembled the hippie free spirit I had met previously. She was in control and eager to explain that the manic incident had caused her so much pain and embarrassment that she hadn't been comfortable talking about her actions with any man, including me. She had worked with a female therapist, but now she was ready to continue with me as her life coach. I was delighted to have her as a new client. We focused on helping her handle her bipolar constructively while setting and achieving career goals. Gabie wanted to be a teacher, so we strategized the best way for her to realize her dreams. She went back to school, earned a master's degree, and is now in the classroom. As long as she stays committed to recovery, I'm confident that Gabie will perform very well. According to her mother, she's doing just that!

Gabie is a good example of the positive things that can happen when people work on their problems. She forgave herself for the issues brought on by her bipolar disorder, and started treatment. She's living a happier, safer, and more fulfilled life because of her healthy decisions.

Although manic episodes can be the most challenging aspects of bipolar disorder, the techniques to control them can be very successful. By combining several strategies—traditional therapy, medication, and support, along with creative endeavors and other training—you can mediate your unnatural highs and keep yourself centered. That requires being under the supervisory care of a physician or therapist so that you have someone to turn to immediately if you feel yourself going into a manic or even depressive phase.

Of course, the goal is to remain episode-free. But if you feel that you're slipping into an all-too-familiar and unwelcome phase, it's much easier to contain the damage if you manage what's happening at an early juncture rather than wait until you're out of control. Many bipolar individuals say that they can definitely notice their moods and energy levels changing as they move into hypomania, that period when the mind starts shifting quickly before it kicks into high gear. The longer people are conscious of their illness, the more attuned they get to those signals. Like me, many patients pay special attention at specific times of the year, since our symptoms seem linked to the changing seasons. I know, for instance, that during spring I have to make sure that I slow down, sleep enough, and watch my spending. I tend to be more energetic during March, April, and May, so I try to limit the potential for a manic episode.

No matter what triggers an episode, your goal will be to slow the process or prevent it from occurring in the first place. Many of the tools below are beneficial whether you're in mania or depression, or in between. They're critical to your well-being!

— **Medications.** Being properly medicated is your best ally in fighting bipolar, particularly a manic cycle. If you're not already on *mood stabilizers,* you need to be evaluated and likely placed on a regimen. People often complain that drugs used to control their racing thoughts and behaviors make them feel "dull" or "flat." I understand the fear of losing your edge because you're on medication. Some bipolar treatments can leave you so sleepy that it's hard to find energy. But I have yet to meet a medical doctor who wants to destroy someone's drive or extinguish someone's inner light or fire.

As a therapist, I certainly didn't want to do that either. I've had a very simple goal for my own bipolar clients: eliminate the parts of the disorder that cause pain and strife, and keep the light burning bright. That means working with a physician to find just the right drug combination and dosage. If what you're taking doesn't seem to work, you likely require an adjustment, either with the drug itself or the prescribed amount. Remember, you're not meant to be a medicated robot who is unable to enjoy fun, experience excitement, or liberate your inner spirit. If you met me, you'd see that I'm passionate about life, even though I take prescriptions several times a day. They haven't dimmed my light. I love the fact that I can meet people and make them laugh. I'm excited that I have the capacity to appreciate everything around me. Like me, when you're in control, you're freed up to enjoy the world!

— **Structure.** Structure and discipline can go a long way in helping you control your thoughts and behaviors. It's important to organize your day, set limits on each activity, and do things in moderation. Whether you're prone to manic free falls or depression, being focused will help you sustain balance.

Because your goal in slowing mania is to stop the racing thoughts and out-of-control behavior, you want to find activities that help you expend your energy but in a very structured, productive way. There are many creative outlets—journaling, drawing, painting, singing, and even writing poetry—that you can tap to satisfy the enormous energy you'll likely have during this phase. The key is to stay within a set timeline. It's dangerous, for instance, to draw for 18 hours but healthy to do it for 1 hour.

The aspiring dancers I went to school with for a time as a youngster in New York City clearly were passionate about their preparation and potential profession. Many of them had dreams of joining professional dance companies, so practicing was key in achieving their goals! But they (or someone close to them) also recognized the limits of their developing bodies. They realized the physical and mental harm of skipping meals and putting off sleep to feed an obsessive practice schedule. Operating at such a fever pitch would put tremendous strain on the body, not to mention stress on the mind. Instead, they danced a few hours a day, leaving time for school, studies, and friends.

Your passions or your dream profession may have nothing do with dance. But as bipolar individuals, we have the best chance of meeting any career or life goal, not to mention satisfying a passion, by being disciplined and structured about it. Focusing on and being excited by something important is a good thing. You want to be persistent and detailed. But it's impossible to maintain the kind of high energy levels many of us experience in mania without crashing, causing harm to our bodies, and disrupting life. You want to meet your objectives, but in a balanced and effective way.

— **Daily exercise.** Research has shown consistently that aerobic or a mix of aerobic and muscle-strengthening activities three to five times a week for 30 to 60 minutes can produce many mental and physical benefits. In terms of bipolar disorder, a one-hour-a-day workout four to five days per week can be a healthy alternative to the intense energy splurge of a manic episode.

The key to remember is that sustained physical activity for longer periods of time is not good. The body can't handle the unhealthy strains bipolar individuals often subject it to during the manic phase. I've known people to jog for hours, swim for days, or Rollerblade all night. They may even exercise extremely hard one day and then avoid the gym for many days.

As long as you maintain a structured regimen, any physical activity will help you release your manic energy, stay calm, and sleep at night. There are many you can do in moderation: run; walk outside; take a class at a gym; use a treadmill; dance; skateboard; or participate in tennis, basketball, soccer, or yoga. (Even if you can't do more than just stretch your limbs because you're incapacitated, exercise them.)

Whatever you do, concentrate. I love to play tennis, not just for the physical benefits and joy of hitting the ball back and forth, but also because I'm focused solely on the game. While I'm playing, I have no worries, challenges, or pain. I just experience the fun of using my body and connecting with another athlete.

— **Meditation and yoga.** Training the mind and body to achieve spiritual awakening and relaxation is a well-respected tradition dating back to the beginning of time. It's also a viable way to balance your bipolar. By incorporating any of the techniques that cultures and religions have used for centuries to achieve tranquility, you center yourself and release your manic and even depressive thoughts.

Meditation, for instance, is a very doable exercise that takes little more on your part than concentration and a quiet place. There are many ways to meditate, but a basic approach involves sitting in a peaceful spot, closing your eyes, slowing your breathing, and consciously clearing your mind. You may even find it useful to tell yourself, *I am calm. I am peaceful. I am slowing down.* Meditating takes practice, but over time it can help you gain clarity while letting go of any overwhelming thoughts.

Likewise, yoga is an effective method of achieving serenity. It involves stretching and posing the body in various positions to achieve strength, flexibility, and tranquility. I suggest investing in a yoga class to realize the full benefits since it can be involved. There are various traditional approaches to this ancient Indian physical and mental discipline. Every movement has a specific purpose and benefit. By working with an instructor, you'll learn how to achieve calm and peace with each pose.

Whether you practice meditation, yoga, or another relaxation technique, there are countless benefits in training the mind and body. If you're bipolar, taking time to focus yourself can slow down your pace. It won't cure your problem, but it can help you feel centered and whole.

— **Breathing, massage, and a warm bath.** The breaths you take can do more than just keep you alive. Controlled breathing exercises are a conscious way to rid yourself of negativity, whether you're fighting a manic attack or depressive episode. How does it work? Each time you breathe in, allow yourself to feel all the negative emotions you're facing. Each time you breathe out, blow the stress, anger, depression, or sadness into the air. By repeating this exercise three times, you gain a sense of calm and peace. If you do it outdoors for a few minutes every day, you'll begin to feel a sense of tranquility. Similarly, having a massage or even taking a warm bath will not only relax your mind and muscles, but also allow you to release your negative thoughts. While bathing I repeat my favorite affirmation: *I am relaxed. I am calm. I feel healthy.* None of these techniques takes the place of your treatment plan, but it can put you in a better emotional place.

— **Sleep.** Sleep plays an important role in your overall health as well as your illness. Although too much sleep is a frequent and debilitating symptom of depression, too little of it can trigger or predict impending mania. In fact, you may be really exhausted, but the inspiration and ideas still keep flowing, so to your mind there's no reason to rest. Instead you push forward with behaviors that can ultimately ruin your reputation, destroy your relationships, or put your finances at risk.

You can greatly benefit from not only monitoring your sleep patterns to gauge what might be happening but also establishing a healthy sleep routine. Getting seven to ten hours of rest a night, for instance, can not only help break those manic cycles but also give your body time to restore energy. Whether or not you have a mental illness, sleep is essential for your well-being. As with food and water, it fuels the energy you need. Without it, you're like a car driving on fumes. You can't operate efficiently. Eventually your mind and body crash.

Sufficient rest, on the other hand, gives your neurons and other cells the chance to repair so that they function efficiently during waking hours. It also keeps your nervous and other systems operating in tip-top shape so that you're alert, able to concentrate, reason, and function. Scientists are still unraveling the mysteries of sleep, including how it figures into bipolar disorder. They know, however, that an established routine of sufficient sleep is important in keeping mood swings in check and preventing relapses. While staying awake for days on end can intensify your manic symptoms, sleeping can bring you down to Earth again.

The Keys to Dealing with Depression

Bipolar depression is more than the lows most people experience periodically during their lives. It's generally a deep, deep sadness that paralyzes you, keeping you from living or functioning normally. Although it manifests differently in each of us, the common thread is to sleep your days away, stop socializing, and give up on your passions. You may hurt so much that you see punching walls, cutting your body, or pounding your head against the door as the only conceivable relief. Since substance abuse is common among sufferers, cocaine, ecstasy, marijuana, or heroin is often the "therapy" of choice to ease the pain.

One of the cruelest aspects of depression is that it feeds on itself. You become upset, which causes you to lose motivation, leading to a decrease in your activities or contact with others. I've watched clients in depressive episodes resign from jobs, quit school, end friendships, leave relationships, and lose interest in every aspect of life because they can't break the downward spiral. They stay in bed for days at a time, which leads to feeling even more depressed and unhappy. Problems seem insurmountable. There's nothing better to do than sleep, and if that doesn't satisfy, contemplate suicide. Life just isn't worth living.

When I first met Todd, he was emotionally broken and in horrible pain. At 45, he felt like 100. He had lost his wife to cancer. He was fired from his Wall Street job. He was facing mounting debts. His children were no longer speaking to him. He didn't see any value to his life other than the amount of money on the insurance policy that his family would inherit. Todd had already attempted suicide five times, using many unimaginable methods: overdosing, carbon monoxide poisoning, and even slitting his wrists. All of them failed. All of them resulted in long hospitalizations.

Despite the deep depression, he desperately wanted help. Over the next two years, he and I met several times a week to work on the long-term emotional issues from childhood that were now hurting his life. After we built a mutual trust, he was able to open up to reveal that he had been abused as a youngster. Because of that, he viewed himself as a disgusting individual who reflexively took the blame for everything. While we worked at changing his negative self-views, he also continued seeing his psychiatrist to regulate his medications.

Todd finally came to accept that his life was valuable and that his past poor choices were directly related to unresolved pain. It became clear to him that he had been hiding from his problems. By the time we finished working together, Todd had turned his life around. His moods were balanced. He had found a new job and was traveling. He was re-building friendships and talking to his children again. He finally saw value in himself beyond just the insurance money his family would inherit. His life wasn't over. He had many reasons to live. In some ways, life had just begun!

As Todd illustrates, depression only gets worse if left untended. Still, it can be reversed or halted in its tracks. With the aid of your doctor, therapist, and medication, your depressive episode doesn't have to spiral. It can be short-lived or not come on at all. The important point is to pay attention to your emotions and take every proactive step possible to keep your depression at bay. Depression doesn't have to leave a lasting mark. You can regain your interest in life with many of the same techniques—taking medications, creating structure, and exercising daily—that help control mania. Also, by adjusting your attitude and focusing on the positive, you'll experience many life-changing secondary gains!

— **Medications.** Just as you need mood stabilizers to bring you into balance, you may also need antidepressants to lift you up. The two types of drugs are often given in conjunction with each other in bipolar, because the risk of switching from depression into full-blown mania increases if you're taking an antidepressant alone.

— **Structure.** Just as you need structure to head off mania, you need structure to fight depression. A daily timetable that forces you to get up, get dressed, eat breakfast, break for lunch, go to the gym, eat dinner, and go to sleep gives you a reason to get out of bed in the morning. The specific times will be unique to you. But by following a set schedule religiously, you'll be up and about, and participating. You'll also experience a level of self-esteem by knowing that you've accomplished even the simplest tasks during the day.

— **Exercise.** Likewise, just as you can use physical activity to redirect your manic energy, you can use it to lift your depression. Exercise boosts the level of the neurochemical *serotonin,* the brain's natural mood enhancer. When serotonin is elevated, depression-related symptoms decrease. In a similar fashion, sustained vigorous exercise promotes *endorphins,* chemicals released from the pituitary gland in response to stressful stimuli. Among their benefits, endorphins diminish the pain associated with exercise, which allows you to go longer and with greater intensity. They also can lessen the effects of stress.

Any activity that gets you out into the elements is good for your emotional health. There are many benefits to connecting with nature, not the least of which is improving your outlook by enjoying the sunlight. (Some studies have even shown that the brain produces more of the mood-lifting serotonin on sunnier, rather than grayer, days.) Take a walk, look at the trees, gaze at the clouds, watch the squirrels, and feel the grass beneath your feet and the sunlight on your face. Realizing that you're part of the larger universe—a world filled with an array of different plants, living creatures, and energy forces—may give you perspective.

Adjust Your Attitude

Since feeling unworthy is so much a part of depression, changing your attitude is critical. I've learned that if you focus on the negative, you only feed the negativity. A pessimistic outlook adds to your struggles; an optimistic one helps you overcome them. I'm often asked why positive people seemingly do better in life than negative people. Does their attitude magically give them an advantage? Yes, if we're talking about the way they respond to life's many blips. A pessimistic person who tries something that doesn't work will likely remark, "I knew it would fail. It's too hard. I give up." But a positive person will look at the same situation with inspiration: "That didn't work out, but if I do something differently, it might. I'll keep trying until it does."

History is brimming with successful people who stayed the course despite many, many blips. Thomas Edison, for instance, tested thousands and thousands of theories and materials before arriving at an efficient incandescent lightbulb. He didn't give up until he discovered that passing electricity through a carbonized cotton filament suspended in a glass vacuum bulb would light the world. We can learn much from Edison's confidence and drive to turn a notion into an invention. If you believe in yourself, it's never too late to achieve your dreams and goals. By changing your thoughts and reality, you can move on with your life, despite your bipolar disorder.

Detail Your Superlatives

When I'm working with depressed clients, I have them create what I call a "what is great about me" board. I pose the question "If we asked all of your family, friends, and others who know you what your good qualities are, what would they say?" The lists are usually litanies of positive adjectives such as "smart," "funny," "creative," "interesting," "honest," "unique," "good [brother, sister, mother, father, daughter, or son]." My clients are generally surprised by the number of superlatives they can list. I then ask, "Do you believe they're true?" They reluctantly say yes. Before they leave my office, I then make sure that they'll repeat the affirmations three times a day.

The beauty of this exercise is that it improves self-esteem, which helps curb depressive thoughts. It's also simple enough to do that you don't need a therapist guiding you. You can create the list and repeat it on your own. It's sometimes tough for bipolar sufferers to truly believe what they're saying initially. (I know. I've been there!) But with practice, you can come to internalize the characteristics you possess. Many of my clients even admit, "I must be a good person if I have so many positive qualities." Yes, they are! So are you!

Suicide Is Never an Option

The potential for suicide actually makes depression a more dangerous cycle than mania. The almost unfathomable statistic linked to bipolar disorder is that one in five people with this mental illness, according to the Depression and Bipolar Support Alliance, are so despondent that they successfully commit suicide. I repeat, *one in five*.[1]

That number is the most important reason why you must overcome your depressive episodes if you're a sufferer, *or* help someone else overcome his or hers if you're a support person.

If you're ever in such a dark place that you might hurt or kill yourself, get help immediately. Call a family member or friend. Seek help from your health care or mental health provider. Talk to your spiritual leader. Contact the National Suicide Prevention Lifeline, which is available 24-7, at 1-800-273-TALK (8255). There may be other organizations in your community that offer the same service and are staffed by volunteers dedicated to help people who are in crisis cope with the moment. Ask your therapist for guidance and keep the number where you can get to it quickly.

If you're an advocate for someone with any mental illness, you also should be aware of suicide-prevention resources in your area. If you think that a friend or loved one is serious about taking his or her life, don't leave that person alone. Stay and get emergency help immediately. If you truly believe a threat is imminent, whether you're experiencing the thoughts yourself or seeing them in someone else, call 911.

There is never a good reason for people with bipolar disorder to end their lives—never! I understand how challenging it is when you're depressed. It's easy to be angry, and convinced that things will never improve. I wanted to give up many times during my five hospitalizations. I didn't like being locked away from my family, friends, and activities. I didn't want to be sick. But I eventually decided to fight. I was willing to do anything and everything to become healthy.

Admitting That You Need to Be Admitted

You may not think that anything positive can come out of a psychiatric hospital, but if your doctor, family member, or someone else admits you, please remember one thing: they're not the enemy. You're being hospitalized because someone who cares about you fears that you're a danger to yourself or others. You can't be alone, because you've lost function or total control. You need to be stabilized with professional help and intense medication, or even *electroconvulsive therapy* (*ECT*).

As draconian as it sounds to stimulate the brain with electrical currents, ECT has been used successfully for decades to treat both manic and depressive phases. Like other therapy, it changes the chemistry of the brain to stabilize a bipolar individual's mood. Only, by sending currents through the brain under anesthesia, this process works faster and more effectively than medications, especially in patients who have been resistant to various combinations.

I tell my clients that, just as a regular hospital is a safety net for patients with life-threatening diseases, a psychiatric hospital is a safety net for patients with potentially harmful mental illnesses. Whatever the emergency, the experience could help you turn a corner or even save your life.

Dale, a bipolar teenager I worked with in therapy, needed intense medication after suffering a psychotic break. He ended up in a New York hospital with which I was affiliated at the time. Dale was hearing voices, thought he was the devil, and even tried to hit himself with a baseball bat. His foster mother was frightened beyond belief. She cared very much about Dale.

After his psychiatrist controlled him with two medications, Dale was calm and willing to work with me in a hospital group and my private practice. Our sessions were intense but very revealing. This intelligent, soft-spoken young man shared a deep, underlying sadness stemming from the sexual abuse he suffered at the hands of other boys in a prior foster home and the rumors they had spread about him being gay. With the help of aggressive treatment, however, Dale overcame his traumas and became a different, self-assured person.

Of course, I've never met anyone who says, "I loved being in that psych ward. When can I go back?" There's no question that it's traumatizing, especially when you come face to face with people like Dale, who are battling their own demons. I didn't enjoy being hospitalized five times in a psychiatric institution. I was just a frightened teenager when I crossed paths with several patients whose disturbing behavior remains carved deeply into my memory: the young girl who beat the crap out of a wall until she could put her fist through it; the grown men who screamed venom and threw chairs until the guards and nurses restrained, medicated, and tied them to their beds; and the 30-something gay guy who put the moves on me until I yelled for help. It was never a pretty scene. I was just discovering who I was and trying to come to grips with my illness when I was locked in this crazy, violent place. I was shell-shocked. It took all of my strength and energy.

I now look back on those experiences as being important in my growth. Because of the first admittance, I learned I had a chronic mental illness, even though I didn't appreciate the news immediately. Because of subsequent admittances, I was stabilized again and again so that I wouldn't harm myself. By observing the errant behaviors of others, I gained a great appreciation of how important it is to be mentally healthy. It obviously took time, since I kept getting readmitted. Yet I came to understand the enormous potential lost when a mind doesn't work properly. I couldn't see the disturbing evidence in myself, but I witnessed it in others. I believe that the pain of those experiences forged me into the husband, father, son, brother, therapist/coach, author, and human being that I am today. The longer I remain stable, the better chance I have of avoiding another psychiatric admission. It's been more than a decade since my last in-hospital "visit." I don't intend to have another one!

. . . .

We all face struggles, traumas, and loss in life, whether or not we're bipolar. The list of things that can go wrong is both long and scary. Yet we have to make peace with painful experiences so that they don't ruin our lives. We all have the power to overcome what comes our way. I believe we're *all* fighters, capable of having outstanding lives, even impacting others. I'm proof that you can triumph over circumstances. With years of therapy, for instance, I learned how to handle the damage that arose from being kidnapped as a child.

When I need inspiration, I often think of another kidnapping victim, Elizabeth Smart, who endured an almost unthinkable ordeal. The Utah teenager was subjected to nine months of daily sexual and other abuse before finally being rescued. Although she could have given up, she survived, not only to testify against her captors but also to advocate for other victims. She's moved on with her life in impressive ways by refusing to let the experience define her or hold her back. She's even found the love of her life and gotten married!

Although my bipolar has manifested mostly in manic symptoms, I've experienced depression at various times, too. I was extremely sad at first learning that I had a lifelong mental illness and had to be hospitalized for it. It took great strength to weather that episode. It was a terrible blow. When one doctor told me I would never completely recover, I had another severe bout. I'm convinced that the heavy emotional baggage of those early events drove me to do everything possible to improve my life.

Today I'm constantly aware that I could lapse into a depressive episode at any time. But I avoid it by being active, working out, and staying positive. I keep my focus every day. You may face the darkest of despair, but you, too, can break free. You can work through whatever has happened or happens in your life. By admitting that you're in a depressive spiral and seeking help, you take the first step in derailing your suicidal thoughts. Just know that brighter days, filled with happiness and hope, are there for you. They're there for all of us if we support each other in healing and staying the course.

Since I know that suicide is a real risk for any bipolar individual, I've also made it my mission to bring the rates among bipolar patients from 1 in 5 to 1 in 100, and finally 0. I encourage you to help me by not becoming a statistic yourself. Life is a gift. It's there for you to enjoy. Live it!

Stoking Your Inner Fire

Finally, whatever techniques you use to create equilibrium in your life, make sure you protect and stoke your *inner fire*. That's the inexplicable force that drives creative and intellectual genius. It's whatever makes you glow from within because you're happy and alive doing it. Finding and pursuing those passions—the skills, talents, and other gifts—that light your inner blaze can be a very positive strategy in dealing with bipolar.

When you're involved with activities that make you happy and fulfilled, you're doing something very constructive with your mind, body, and time. Perhaps it's dancing, writing, or public speaking. Maybe it's teaching, traveling, or playing sports. Whatever makes you feel alive, you can use to further your recovery.

I know that sometimes it's difficult to imagine even having dreams, ambitions, or passions, given the adversities of a mental illness. I've had those feelings often. For a long time, others believed I was doing very well given that I was living on my own and not in a group home. I, on the other hand, thought I was still sick. I was just surviving, but that was enough since it was too much work to believe otherwise. I finally realized that I was meant to achieve *every* goal that God had placed in my mind and heart. Although my fire had dimmed, I was able to reignite it. I would learn over time that I still needed to keep the flames burning brightly in a healthy, effective way.

Today I tell my clients to imagine their inner blaze as a glowing campfire. If built correctly and tended carefully, it's cozy and inviting. It illuminates. It warms. (And it's a darned good place to roast hot dogs and s'mores.) But if the campfire grows too large or is left unattended, it can spread like wildfire, engulfing everything in its path. Our passions are similar to that campfire. We need to stay within healthy boundaries, or we wreak havoc on anything or anyone around us. Some of us try to fuel the flame, so to speak, with alcohol or drugs, even though the outcome isn't at all pretty. But those of us who have learned to stoke our inner flame carefully have benefited from a sustained glow.

When I'm not seeing clients, I love writing. Whether I'm journaling or fine-tuning a manuscript, I let my creative juices flow for hours on end. When I'm putting words to paper or computer screen, I feel complete. In the past, however, I would write for ten hours a day. I'd sometimes stay up all night, fueled only by black coffee and my mania. I believed my creative fires were burning hot. (I even thought of my writing as sexy!) But I was simply out of control. I was irritable, agitated, and just plain ugly to be around. I'd be rude to my mother and anyone else who invaded my space or couldn't keep up with my racing thoughts or lightning speed. Then I had trouble calming down. When I finally could sleep, I was so tired that I'd be out for hours.

I was pursuing my passion all right, but destructively. I eventually accepted that slow and steady works much better than fast and furious. Now I keep my inner fire burning brightly by writing at a more productive and healthy pace. I also feel passion and joy with my wife, my daughter, and my work. I take chances. I go on adventures. I feel alive again. The difference between then and now is that I control my fire in all things. It no longer controls me! My light glows brightly. That's what I wish for *you.*

One Final Note

You need to attack your bipolar disorder with every weapon in your arsenal. It's not enough to get medicated without addressing your emotional issues or to undergo therapy without changing your daily life. Manic depression is a complicated illness that usually involves a matrix of problems. Addressing one but not the others won't produce the kind of results you need to lead a healthy, normal life. The beauty (and yes, I say *beauty*) of this disorder is that you can control much of your own recovery. You make positive changes by *choosing* to see the right mental health professionals, *choosing* to get medicated correctly, and *choosing* to make modifications in the way you conduct business. When you're willing to commit to all three weapons, you can make lasting progress. You can put yourself on the road to recovery.

● ● ●

CHAPTER FOUR

TALK THERAPY

IF YOU HAVE bipolar, you don't want to suffer in silence. Believe me, isolation is not your friend. Going it alone can shortchange your recovery by keeping you from the very professionals who can improve your life.

Tapping a skilled mental health professional to help you navigate the turbulent waters of your illness can add much-needed ballast, or stability, to your often-adrift ship. A psychologist, social worker, or other practitioner can steer you with the guidance and perspective that you can't possibly give yourself. He or she does so by teaching you how to come to grips with your past, let go of your pain, and deal positively with your illness.

I know it can be daunting. The hurts related to this and other mental illnesses may be so ingrained in your mind and spirit that it's hard to imagine how *talk therapy* or *psychotherapy* will help. The journey from unhealthy to healthy can be frightening and riddled with unknowns.

Yet there are many positives in engaging a mental health professional, not the least of which is that you have a partner in your struggles. On its own, therapy is a powerful technique for dealing with the ramifications of your bipolar disorder. But when combined with medication and group support, talking with a mental health professional can have a synergistic effect. One approach enhances the other in boosting your recovery.

I believe you will get the most out of treatment if you attack your illness with every relevant weapon: drugs to correct the biochemical imbalance in your brain, group support to provide a safety net, and talk therapy to address your issues.

I know there are exceptions to the rule. Not everyone requires or can afford intense therapy over months, if not years. People vary in their needs, ability to pay, and willingness to commit. Yet the longer you can remain in a productive therapeutic relationship, the more you'll gain from the experience. It can change your world. I know. It did for me.

Not only did Dr. Amy Koreen prescribe a drug combination that finally stabilized me and gave me hope, but she also convinced me that I had to do more than take my meds to keep my bipolar in check. For the first time, after years of disruptive behavior, I agreed to see a therapist regularly, stick with my medication regimen, and take care of myself physically. I needed to eat well, exercise, and get plenty of sleep so that my body had a chance to heal. With Dr. Amy's help, I learned that small steps and slow, steady progress would give me the best chance to regain my footing, sanity, and life.

If you're ready to regain your own footing, sanity, and life, therapy will be key. Working with a mental health professional can help you accomplish several goals: come to terms with your illness and its repercussions, understand and forgive your past episodes, and anticipate the stressors in your life that may trigger or intensify your symptoms. Whatever your objective, by engaging a mental health professional, you won't have to fly solo!

Therapy as Team Sport

Treating bipolar disorder requires a team of health professionals using an arsenal of tools. The good news is that various providers can assist you with your disorder. They may differ in their training, approaches, and even specific roles, but mental health professionals who work with bipolar patients usually understand the intricate challenges of the illness and have many techniques that work.

— **Psychiatrists.** If you've been officially diagnosed with bipolar disorder, you've probably already encountered a psychiatrist. With medical degrees and specialized training in diseases of the mind, they're usually the go-to professionals for a mental diagnosis. Because they are trained as physicians, however, they're also licensed to prescribe *psychotropic* medications. Your psychiatrist can find the best drug combination for you, just as Dr. Amy did for me. Once you're diagnosed, your only encounter with this person may be in monitoring and adjusting your meds. Even though many psychiatrists also do psychotherapy, you'll likely have to tap the therapy talents of others, depending on the severity of your illness and the limits of your insurance coverage.

— **Clinical psychologists.** Although they're also referred to as "Dr.," these mental health professionals have earned a *Ph.D.* or *Psy.D.* rather than an *M.D.* or *D.O.* They've pursued graduate studies in psychology, focusing on the mind in relation to behavior. Among their skills, clinical psychologists are adept at conducting psychological testing, which may aid in diagnosis. In some states they're also licensed to prescribe medications. Their usual role with bipolar individuals, however, is to conduct psychotherapy. For that, they're eminently qualified.

— **Clinical and psychiatric social workers.** Mental health professionals who practice as social workers must hold a master's degree in order to be licensed as a therapist and be reimbursed for their efforts. That involves two years of a supervised internship in addition to graduate course work. Social workers perform many of the same counseling functions as psychologists in that they, too, meet privately with clients, conduct group therapy, work with families, and collaborate with psychiatrists over care. In addition to staffing all sorts of institutions, they also may have their own private practices, focusing on patients with mental health problems such as bipolar disorder.

Before I became a life coach, I parlayed my master's degree in social work from New York's Adelphi University, Long Island, into private practice. Although my focus with bipolar patients then was therapeutic in nature, my work now involves setting and meeting broader life and career agendas. That doesn't mean I've set aside my social work training and therapeutic intuition, however. I often rely on those original skills and observations to help clients work through roadblocks to success.

Besides a psychiatrist, clinical psychologist, or social worker, you may tap other counseling professionals to help you navigate your bipolar disorder. *Psychiatric nurse practitioners,* for instance, are registered nurses who have earned master's degrees and sometimes Ph.D.'s to work as advanced mental health nurses. They, too, can counsel patients and prescribe medication, either independently or in collaboration with a physician. Whatever the educational background, the important strategy is to find someone qualified who matches your style and personality. You need to ask the following questions in your search.

What to Ask Your Clinician

— **"How much do you charge, and will you take my insurance?"** These may be game changers. No matter how bad your bipolar, you have to deal with the practicalities of long-term care. Costs vary widely among therapists, depending on their training and years of experience. A psychiatrist or psychologist will likely charge a higher rate per hour than a social worker or other mental health provider. Don't assume, however, that rate equals competence. You can find many fine practitioners in each of the professional categories discussed in the previous section. The caveat, however, is that if you have severe symptoms or a complex medical history, you may need the higher-priced therapy services of a psychiatrist for more than just monitoring your medications.

Whomever you select, make sure you have a discussion about perhour fees and third-party reimbursement. You need to know up front what your insurance policy allows and if the clinician is on the provider list. If you don't have the means to pay, ask your doctor for a referral to a local free clinic. (Or check out the Depression and Bipolar Support Alliance website at **www.dbsalliance.org**.) Although there may be a waiting list, and you may have to see someone who doesn't specialize in bipolar, you'll at least be under the care of a mental health professional.

— **"Are you licensed by the state?"** Licensure means that a mental health provider has met minimum competencies or standards to practice in your state. That includes completing training and amassing experience and expertise in the field. Licensure doesn't ensure quality, but it does mean the person has covered the basics and may be qualified to help you.

— **"How long have you been in practice?"** Longevity in the profession isn't necessarily *the* most important criterion for picking a mental health professional, since someone just coming out of training and building a client base could be a fabulous fit. On the other hand, nothing substitutes for experience in any profession, especially this one. Someone who's been in the trenches, so to speak, in treating bipolar disorder will understand it in every way.

— **"How much do you work with bipolar patients?"** Seeing someone with a wide spectrum of other clients rather than a sole focus on bipolar patients may or may not be a game changer for you. There are many common threads in treating mental health issues, no matter what the underlying diagnosis. Yet therapists are usually good at a few things, not necessarily everything. So finding someone who targets bipolar disorder and its related illnesses can be vital in your progress. A therapist who has the nuanced skills, experience, and success with similar patients may be successful with you, too.

— **"How would you describe your approach and work style with patients?"** Therapists have many techniques and tools to use with clients who have bipolar disorder. Some schools of thought are more scientifically based than others. There's no one-size-fits-all approach to psychotherapy, but *cognitive behavioral therapy,* or *CBT,* is a mainstay. Although it can be adapted for a variety of mental disorders, including bipolar, CBT basically involves reeducating the mind. Patients learn how to identify distorted thoughts, beliefs, and behaviors, and then change them. CBT can help you not only to cope with your symptoms and stick with treatment, but also to deal with life in positive ways.

Your therapist may suggest a treatment plan that combines several approaches, depending on your evolving needs. You don't have to know all of the options, but you should have a general idea of what this person anticipates. At the very least, ask about the interaction during your sessions: does the therapist want to engage in active dialogue, or just be quiet and offer limited response until the end? Either style is valid, but if you're the silent type, you may need prompting. Then again, maybe you want this time to vent and are just fine hearing a summary in the end. In either case, it's helpful to have a sense of what techniques a therapist might use. It's part of making the right match.

— **"If you're not a medical doctor, do you work with one who can manage my medications?"** It's important that your therapist have a relationship with a psychiatrist or other physician so that if you need to be on medication, you'll get it. Most legitimate therapists have such ties. Conversely, a psychiatrist who has diagnosed you probably can refer you to a mental health professional on his or her go-to list.

— **"What's your appointment availability, and what happens if I have to cancel?"** If you can only come on Thursday nights or Saturday mornings, and the therapist is booked with evening regulars or doesn't see people on weekends, you'll have to look further. Since many people want after-work appointments, they're usually in high demand. It's important to find a therapist who can accommodate you at the same time each week, however, so that it becomes a regular part of your life. Also, some counselors charge for missed appointments and cancellations. Make sure you understand the ground rules, especially if you're dependent on others to get you to your sessions.

— "**Do you have a backup if you're not available and I have an emergency?**" Just as it's important for your general physician to be part of an on-call network, it's important for your therapist to have similar colleagues for cover. How does it work? Who would you call for immediate help? You may not anticipate future problems, but if you're in crisis or just need an extra appointment, you'll want to know what to do next.

You'll likely have many other questions. The important point is to have a face-to-face meeting so that you can gauge your interaction. Research has consistently shown that a good therapeutic outcome relies as much on the fit between therapist and patient as it does on the approach. On paper, this person may be the best match for you, and you may be the best match for him or her. But sometimes the collaboration just doesn't work.

If you're having difficulty relating, discuss it. If the two of you can't agree on an accommodation, don't be afraid to move on. There's nothing wrong with changing course. In my own bipolar journey, I've had therapists who didn't work out and those with whom I was both comfortable and very satisfied. I encourage you to seek out that special individual with whom you click.

Coaching for Life

You may want to tap one other group of experts in re-crafting your life. As part of an emerging field, *life coaches* work with clients to help them set, track, and achieve professional and personal goals. Although training guru Tony Robbins has given a face to the field, most life coaches, including me, are low profile in the way we assist clients. I even like to think of the job that I now do as similar to that of a personal trainer. In this case, however, we're not just worried about altering someone's physique and physical well-being. We're focused on improving all aspects of a person's life.

This field is different from psychotherapy, especially in terms of bipolar disorder, in that it's not the job of a life coach to help clients work through the emotional issues related to their mental illness. That's the job of a therapist. Even though some of us have extensive backgrounds in psychology, social work, or a related field, we're committed to a more universal goal: to motivate people to reach for and achieve each of their family, health, and career objectives.

In my case, several years ago I chose to focus exclusively on coaching bipolar individuals and their families to take the positive, practical steps necessary to lead a normal, productive life. That's not to say that I don't listen or don't draw upon my years as a psychotherapist or even my own illness. (One of the benefits of being a life coach rather than an active therapist is that I can share aspects of my own condition when I think it might help—hence this entire book!) I often use what I learned from my traditional practice. My role today, however, is largely to advise, motivate, and connect clients with resources. If they need therapy, for instance, I refer them to licensed professionals. If their families need help, I coordinate care, identify treatment options, and deal with the myriad struggles related to this illness. (I also train others to do the same.) Whatever the request, I find great satisfaction in meeting it with them. I'm doing what I was meant to do: coaching others with bipolar to help them move forward with their lives!

Meeting You on Your Turf

Although there are many different psychotherapeutic techniques, they largely rest on the same concept: building mutual trust to facilitate honest dialogue or exchange. In fact, the key is to freely communicate what's in your heart and mind so that your therapist can help you work through your issues and arrive at doable solutions.

Even if you have difficulty expressing yourself verbally, it's important to put your emotions on the table. A mental health professional who is familiar with bipolar disorder and trained in various psychotherapy techniques can draw you out, analyze your moods, evaluate your behavior, and help you modify what needs to change.

Whether your counselor asks many questions or lets you just talk, he or she is trained to deal with any response, including your anger, ambivalence, hesitancies, and even denial. As a therapist, I often saw initial reluctance on the part of clients to share honest and sometimes very raw emotions. When they saw, however, that my only purpose was their improvement, they usually relaxed. They even found joy in knowing that they could make changes. My life-coaching clients often exhibit similar hesitancies. Even though they engage me to meet very specific career and personal goals, it takes a while for them to get comfortable, too. Once they do, they're surprised by their progress.

Whatever the approach, a good counselor is flexible enough to adjust and respond to your fluctuating moods and behaviors. He or she meets you where you are that day. Even as a life coach, I never begin with my own agenda when working with clients. First I want to get a sense of what this person needs from me, not what I need from him or her. Whether it's a topic we've covered in the past or one that has surfaced since our last appointment, I'm flexible. I like to think that three of the qualities I bring to my work are a calm, soothing demeanor; the ability to remember details; and the capacity to tailor each session. I'm in the moment, as they say, ready to go where this person needs and wants to go. That's what you want from your mental health professional. He or she can also offer you the following:

— **A safe haven for healing thorny family issues.** Because therapists don't live with the relatives of their patients, they usually can bring a fresh perspective to any situation. They offer a secure place to work through knotty issues involving family members. The solution might be to mend the relationships, to find coping mechanisms for living with the parties, or to simply walk away. But a therapist can help you sort through the options. For instance, a common complaint from my therapy clients was that family members didn't value them because of their bipolar. Perhaps a sibling taunted them mercilessly, or fights were never resolved their way. As the objective party, I could help them sort through the facts, either validating their feelings or telling them nicely that they were off base. My clients could talk freely as I helped them organize their thoughts and craft measured responses. Whatever the level of anger, they would vent in my office to avoid erupting at home.

— **A safe place to grow into your own.** Sometimes the best role a mental health professional plays is in helping patients redefine their relationships. I know it's difficult to stretch beyond the comfort zone of parents and siblings. They've listened to our fears and helped us work through our feelings about being bipolar. But at some point as young adults, we need to find our own way. (I meet 40-year-olds who are in the unfortunate situation of still wanting the approval of their mothers.) It's a healthy passage of life when parents let go of children *and* children let go of parents. Of course, if they've been there for you in the past, they'll be there for you in the future. But your therapist can help you define new roles.

When I wanted to leave my native New York for California, I knew I needed a perspective other than my mom's. I adore her but was aware that she'd have a very difficult time giving me unbiased advice. She didn't want me to leave. My therapist, on the other hand, helped me work through the questions I needed to ask about this decision. Our conversation validated my intense interest in following my dreams, even if they took me to the West Coast. Today my mother and I live thousands of miles apart, but we're still very much connected. I speak with her often. We share what's going on in our separate lives. We support each other emotionally. My choice to move on may have been uncomfortable for both of us at the time, but she's never wavered in her love and support.

De-stressing Together

It's no secret that bipolar disorder can take aim at an entire family. As primary caregivers, parents and siblings are critical in helping patients manage their illness. Yet family members often bear the brunt of a loved one's chronic illness without support. What's more, research consistently shows that caregivers suffer unique stresses that make them prone to illness, too. Separate studies put them at higher risk for developing sleep problems and chronic health issues such as high blood pressure and bouts of depression.

Family-focused therapy, or *FFT,* helps both patients and their caregivers work through the issues that are causing tension. The idea is to come together to identify any conflicts that may be affecting your illness and find ways to resolve them. That may involve reeducating parents and siblings about the illness so that they're better equipped to spot a relapse and implement an action plan to deal with it. It can also include defusing any hostility or unhelpful criticisms due to everyone's frustrations.

Unlike individual therapy, FFT is a joint operation. Patients and family members attend appointments together, even though the therapist may have to perform discussion jujitsu to make sure everyone's needs are met. The triple hope is that caregivers learn to accept how the disorder affects and possibly even limits their bipolar loved ones, loved ones take responsibility for their well-being and actions, and both parties find better coping mechanisms to deal with each other. Studies have shown that family-focused therapy can help stabilize the illness and avoid relapses. There's a good likelihood that it can help you and your family, too.

Make the Commitment

Therapy is only as good as the effort you put into it. If you're silent during your sessions or cover up your real concerns, you'll never solve your issues. The feedback won't be worth your time and money unless you're open and engaged. So how can you get the most out of every session? It's not rocket science, but it takes commitment first, followed by a few simple steps:

— **Attend all of your sessions.** Being sloppy about therapy will get you nowhere with your therapist. If you're committed to getting healthy, you'll want to make all of your appointments *and* be on time. Reliability shows that you're committed to the cause and willing to move mountains to make progress. You'll also be more productive once you're in session, because the two of you don't have to address your absences or tardiness.

— **Be honest.** Therapists work best when their clients are open about everything. The only way you can make positive progress is to tell this person everything you're feeling, even if it involves paranoia, hallucinations, or urges to hurt someone. Mental health professionals are trained to take in anything you say and respond in a nonjudgmental, objective, and helpful way. You aren't there to impress anyone, so don't hold back or lie. Take advantage of the fact that this is a private session. Reputable psychiatrists, psychologists, social workers, and other mental health providers operate under strict professional codes of ethics as well as federal laws, principally the Health Insurance Portability and Accountability Act, or HIPAA. Both demand confidentiality. (As noted in the front of this book, the stories in this book have been modified to protect the privacy of clients.) You should have no worries about expressing all your concerns. Remember, there are no right or wrong answers, just truthful ones.

— **Talk about your life as well as your bipolar.** Since mental illness can affect every aspect of your day and being, it's essential that you share what's going on with family, relationships, and work or school. Your therapist will use the information to analyze where you are in terms of the illness and what you might have to do next. Also, since bipolar often occurs in conjunction with other major problems, such as alcoholism and drug abuse, you'll need to be honest about those conditions, too. In either case, don't hold back.

— **Focus on any past pain.** Clinging to the hurts of your life will only hold you back from a positive future. The purpose of therapy is not only to understand the repercussions of your episodes but also to work out any underlying issues. Refusing to admit that you've been abused; faced psychiatric commitments; or been hurt by deep, dark family secrets will continue to haunt you. Harboring the pain may even take you to the darkest of places, contemplating suicide. But if you're willing to find coping mechanisms or closure for past indiscretions, incidents, and issues, you can move forward with hope and light.

— **Share every emotion.** It doesn't benefit you to hold back your anger and pain. Even if you raise your voice or beat a pillow during your session, it's vital to unleash your feelings: cry, scream, let your anger out. It's a healthy part of the process. As embarrassed as you might be about losing control, if you're doing it in the safety of a therapy session, your counselor can help you make sense of it all. Once you've vented, you'll be able to explore your grief and anger. Being strong and silent may be appropriate under other circumstances, but in the context of therapy, it's okay to let it rip. You'll likely feel relief!

— **Know your stressors.** To make progress with your illness, it's good to know how your mind works. I don't mean taking a PET scan to see how it's physiologically functioning. I mean tracking certain patterns that might be key to your episodes. What are your biggest fears? What causes you to react negatively? What harmful ideas crop up again and again? Your counselor obviously can't climb into your head to switch off your thinking. Yet with approaches such as cognitive behavioral therapy, he or she can help you retool your thoughts and behavior.

— **Ask questions.** If you need clarification or advice on handling specific situations, make sure you follow up with a question. Whether your concerns center on a family member at home, bullying at school, or any other issue, everything about you is on the table. So don't be afraid to ask!

— **Listen carefully to the advice and take it.** Good therapists have effective techniques for helping you deal with your bipolar. They're schooled in a variety of approaches to assist clients in addressing their pain and making life-altering choices. It's up to you, though, to take the advice and implement it in your daily life. You're not in therapy just to talk and listen. You're there to take action. It may take time to stop your addictions, reconfigure your thinking, and get rid of your anxieties. But by being faithful with your sessions and practicing what you learn, you have a good chance of recovery. I've seen clients drop weight, as well as stop drinking, smoking, and doing drugs, just by heeding the strategies and advice of a therapist. You can experience similar great results!

— **Make sure you're satisfied.** If you feel that you and your therapist are not simpatico, then don't be afraid to move on. Mental health professionals differ in style, personality, and approach. Some work only with bipolar individuals, while others focus on their families and support persons. Some like to narrow their practices to adults, while others deal only with adolescents. Whatever your specific need, if you don't think it's a good fit even after one or two sessions, then it's time to look further. As a professional who has your best interests at heart, your therapist likely will be of the same mind. He or she may even make a referral to someone with whom you'll click.

— **Thank your mental health professional by learning, growing, and making positive changes.** Your therapist's goal is to help you become the best person you can be. No matter what baggage you bring to each session, your counselor is dedicated and trained to help you understand your thoughts and modify your behavior. Your growth is this person's fulfillment. So make it worthwhile for you both. Work hard, stay committed, and reach for your goals.

Therapy by Group

Your doctor may suggest group therapy as an adjunct to your private sessions. Meeting with others can be a positive experience in that you get the immediate feedback of a mental health professional as well as observations from others who are facing the same problems. If you've been hospitalized, it's very likely that your treatment included one or even more group sessions, depending on your ancillary issues. Continuing that experience on the outside can be very productive. There's one caveat, however: you may not be a group candidate if your behavior could endanger others or you're prone to severe anxiety attacks. Your physician may suggest holding off until it's safe for both you and them.

Also, don't confuse group therapy with a support group. They are different animals with different purposes, even though both can be essential to your mental health recovery. A self-help support group offers an opportunity to socialize and share with others like you. It supplements all of the other things you're doing to get healthy. But it's not designed to delve deeply into the complicated issues connected to your illness. It's there primarily to help you break the isolation of your mental illness by joining like-minded people. Many of my clients have enjoyed combining all of these modalities to get the best of every world: individual help, group discussion, and continuing support.

. . . .

Taking Your Concerns Elsewhere

Not all patients want to participate in psychotherapy. Some individuals choose, for instance, to work through their problems via their religious beliefs. I won't judge people for joining a monastery, traveling to India, or taking any other faith journey in search of a solution or inner peace. I can only say that psychotherapy and medication have worked miracles for my clients and me. We're all entitled to make our own choices. Yet if bipolar is ruining your life, you need to get a handle on your illness. It's incumbent upon you to figure out what works best and pursue it.

Likewise, not everyone will want to continue therapy or be able to do so. Insurance plans vary significantly in what they'll cover for psychotherapy, which may make it difficult for you if you can't carry the full freight. Your therapist can help you decide how to get the most out of your time together and keep progressing if you can't meet once or several times a week. One option may be to seek free clinic services in your community. Whatever you do, make sure that if you leave therapy, you have a support system in place.

One Final Note

My mental health team has played an enormous role in my life. I've worked with more than 20 physicians, therapists, and life coaches since I first got help in handling my parental abduction as a child. It took some time to identify a therapist initially to deal specifically with my bipolar. Yet once I connected, I felt safe enough to share feelings I didn't even want to tell family and friends about. Today I meet regularly with my own life coach. I consider it an important plus, since I'm forever refining my life!

However extensive your formal therapy, I guarantee that if you work at it, you *will* grow. The more open you are with your concerns and fears, the more valuable the lessons you'll learn and the more progress you'll make. Whether you experience gradual growth or *Aha!* moments, you *will* attain wisdom and a deeper understanding of yourself and your disorder. You *will* strengthen your inner resolve in ways that will help you handle the major challenges and disappointments of life. I promise. I've been there. I wish the same result for you!

●　●　●

CHAPTER FIVE

MEDICATING YOUR SWINGS

BIPOLAR DISORDER IS a real illness that needs real medication. Because research has consistently shown that the most successful treatment is an integrated approach with a trifecta of tools (therapy, drugs, and support), you don't want to shortchange yourself by refusing a drug regimen. No matter how severe your bipolar, it's critical that you get properly medicated.

Unfortunately, bipolar patients often don't see it that way. They're overwhelmed by the process and, in some ways, justifiably so. Finding the right combination of the drugs—*mood stabilizers* (antiseizure or anticonvulsant drugs), *antipsychotics,* and *antidepressants*—available today is a trial-and-error process that demands persistence. Everyone responds differently, so hitting on a formula that might work long-term will likely take weeks, if not months. Even then, the medications for bipolar disorder often generate bothersome, even nasty, side effects, so taking them isn't a walk in the park.

As I tell clients, however, if you want to survive cancer, you'd take your medicine, with all of its painful side effects, just to save your life. Wouldn't you? Of course you would! Bipolar disorder won't kill you in the same way that malignant cells multiplying at catastrophic rates can physically snuff out your life. But if left untreated, this mental illness can derail your moods and destroy your spirit, not to mention put you on a very unhealthy path.

Of course, it's your right to reject advice from your physician, including the strong suggestion that you need a prescription. But as someone who has lived with bipolar disorder and watched others do the same, I can tell you that choosing the delusions of full-blown mania or the suicidal thoughts of deep depression over sanity, stability, and a shot at a normal life is *not* a good choice. It will likely lead you to the hospital or to an even darker place.

The reality of this disease is that if you aren't faithful in continuing drug treatment, you run the real risk of relapsing or having minor mood changes turn into full-blown manic or depressive episodes. I can't stress enough the importance of maintenance medication in sustaining your mental health. Therapy and a support network are necessary components—no question about it. Yet, the right medication combination can do what they physiologically can't do: work on your brain biochemically to keep your moods and emotions in balance. No amount of talking can do that!

Lithium, the Original Mood Stabilizer

You may or may not have experience with bipolar medications, depending on where you are in confronting your illness. But rest assured that because of today's pharmacology, psychiatrists have a stable of prescription drugs to keep you balanced and out of the hospital. *Mood stabilizers* provide the cornerstone for all bipolar therapy. They're go-to medications because they're effective in bringing and keeping manic-depressive episodes under control by reversing and preventing the extreme highs and lows (hence the term *mood stabilizer!*).

Bipolar patients have *lithium carbonate* (or simply *lithium*) to thank for providing frustrated clinicians with the first therapeutically effective medication in the mood-stabilizer family. Until the Food and Drug

Administration (FDA) approved this breakthrough remedy in 1970, patients had a rough time addressing the stubborn nature of their manic depression.

Before then, doctors and patients relied on other therapies and approaches. Until the early 1950s, for instance, the only real treatment for patients prone to a psychotic episode was long-term hospitalization. Whatever was causing the attacks, patients had to be institutionalized to deal with them. Once *Thorazine,* a first-generation antipsychotic medication, entered the U.S. market in 1952, however, doctors finally had an outpatient schizophrenia drug that worked on people with any psychosis, including the deep throes of manic depression. But it also produced severe side effects, as did subsequent antipsychotic medications.

First in Effectiveness

Lithium carbonate was a breath of therapeutic fresh air. When it finally appeared on the scene, lithium freed individuals from the severe disruptions and profound withdrawals of their bipolar symptoms, without the crippling side effects. More important, by stabilizing moods, the drug also gave individuals the balanced presence of mind necessary to delve into their psychological issues. With a clear head and the help of therapists, many manic-depressive individuals finally could confront what they needed to face to be healthy.

Gold from Salt

Lithium carbonate remains the "gold standard" and the most commonly used drug to treat bipolar disorder. Chemically speaking, it's kith and kin to common table salt. More specifically, it's a derivative of the naturally occurring soft, silver-white metallic substance *lithium,* represented by the symbol *Li* or number 3 on the periodic table of chemical elements. Produced in nature from many minerals, lithium is medically effective in its salt form and as a chemical compound, either *lithium carbonate* or *lithium citrate.*

Australian psychiatrist John Cade first suggested in 1949 that lithium could treat depressive-type illnesses. He and subsequent scientists demonstrated that it could calm manic symptoms effectively without producing the characteristic sedating effects of first-generation antipsychotic medications. It took the next 20 years to prove to the FDA that lithium was neither a fluke nor completely toxic to the body. Patients who tolerated and stayed on the drug experienced demonstrable relief.

Even today, scientists aren't certain how this trailblazer medication actually stabilizes a person's mood swings. The strong sense, however, is that it diminishes excessive electrical activity in the central nervous system (the brain and spinal cord) by affecting the neurotransmitters in some yet-to-be-discovered way. Whatever the mechanism, the drug produces results on both cycle fronts. It not only lessens the intensity and frequency of manic episodes but also prevents or lifts depression.

Effective, Not Perfect

As with other medications, however, lithium has its drawbacks. Because the drug takes several weeks to produce noticeable results, you may be on a short course of another medication, such as a *rapidly acting antipsychotic,* to jump-start your recovery. People on lithium are also likely to experience such side effects as slight nausea; stomach cramps; diarrhea; thirstiness; muscle weakness; and feelings of being dazed, tired, or sleepy, which may or may not continue over time.

The real issue with lithium is toxicity. You may not be able to tolerate the medication from the get-go, because it's either not right for your body or another condition precludes you from taking it. Even if the drug is for you, lithium is unusual in that the amount necessary to be effective is slightly less than the amount that makes it toxic. In other words, small changes to your daily routine or major changes in your health—especially if they result in dehydration—can alter the way the drug behaves.

Tending Lithium

Your psychiatrist will insist on periodic blood testing to determine if you're getting enough or too much of the drug. Levels that are too low can lead to a relapse. Levels that are too high can result in various debilitating effects. Lithium medication is a salt, which means it dissolves in water. Why is that important? You may experience toxicity if you're dehydrated or taking other medications that lead to dehydration, since dangerously high levels of the drug then build up or concentrate in your blood. That can lead to a number of symptoms:

- Extreme thirst and frequent urination

- Severe nausea, vomiting, or persistent diarrhea

- Shaking, muscle twitching, jerking or restless limbs, or hand trembling

- Eye pain

- Blurred or double vision

- Persistent headache

- Marked dizziness, loss of balance, or difficulty walking

- Slurred speech

- Feeling light-headed or faint

- Slow or irregular heartbeat

- Swelling of the feet or lower legs

- Weakness

- Confusion, hallucinations, or seizures

If you have any of the above symptoms, you need to stop the medication, drink lots of water, and see your physician immediately. Even if drug levels aren't toxic, these side effects suggest that your lithium level is too high or that the medication isn't the right one for you. Since lithium can cause thyroid problems and, in rare cases, damage the kidneys, you'll need to watch your diet, track your salt intake, be careful about caffeine and tea consumption, monitor your weight gains or losses, and be cautious in taking other prescription and over-the-counter medications. Drugs such as ibuprofen, diuretics, and heart and blood-pressure medication, for instance, can affect the action of lithium.

The bottom line is that lithium must be taken with care and adjusted when necessary. If your doctor can get you stabilized with the proper dosage, however, you may not need another medication. Many people control their bipolar with this drug alone. Whatever combination your doctor recommends, lithium can be a powerful weapon.

Lithium is sold under several brand names, including:

- Eskalith

- Lithobid

- Lithonate

- Lithotabs

Lithium is usually administered orally.

A Stable of Other Mood Stabilizers

Except for lithium, today's mood stabilizers usually come from a class of drugs known as *anticonvulsants*. Normally used for treating epi-

leptic and other seizures, these medications have proved to be successful in both controlling manic symptoms and reducing bipolar swings.
When first approved by the FDA in 1995, *valproic acid* (or its sodium salt,
valproate, or a compound of both, *divalproex sodium*) gave physicians and
their bipolar patients a highly effective *antimanic* alternative to lithium.
It's often a first-choice drug for individuals suffering from rapid cycling,
mixed mania, or mania with hallucinations or delusions.

Today's anticonvulsants slow down the firing rates of *neurons,* the basic building blocks or cells of the nervous system so that the brain is not
overly excited. They do so via several mechanisms, including blocking
specific channels responsible for the firings or increasing levels of GABA,
the brain's most abundant inhibitory neurotransmitter. Anticonvulsants
can be very successful in lessening the likelihood of a manic or depressive
episode. At the same time, they can cause a variety of symptoms:

- Cold-like symptoms

- Constipation, diarrhea, or nausea

- Dizziness

- Drowsiness

- Headache

- Heartburn

- Mild hair loss

- Tremors

Your doctor will want to keep close tabs on your blood counts, not
just to monitor the effectiveness of the medication but also to ensure
that you're not doing damage to your body. Mood stabilizers can cause
liver damage. One drug, *Tegretol* (*cabamazepine*), can also lead to dangerously reduced red and white blood cells. This situation, albeit rare,

manifests as sore, ulcerated gums, along with flu-like symptoms. The symptoms go away once the medication is stopped. With regular tracking, your psychiatrist can make sure you're within acceptable cell-count range.

Anticonvulsant or antiseizure medications used as mood stabilizers are sold under several brand names based on their unique formulations. They include:

- Depakote (valproic acid or divalproex sodium)

- Depakene (valproic acid or divalproex sodium)

- Tegretol (cabamazepine)

- Lamictal (lamotrigne)

- Topamax (topiramate)

Like lithium, mood stabilizers are usually administered orally several times a day.

Atypical Antipsychotics

Your doctor may put you on what's called a *second-generation* (or *atypical*) *antipsychotic*. Drugs in this category are frequently ordered if you're experiencing sudden or severe mania, or psychosis. They may also be prescribed to stabilize your mood until your other medication kicks in or in place of an anticonvulsant if none of them work. These drugs are excellent for mixed-episode relief.

Like first-generation antipsychotics, atypical antipsychotics work by blocking or lessening the action of *serotonin* and *dopamine*, two specific neurotransmitters or chemicals within nerve cells tasked with shuttling messages between the cells. They're known catalysts in regulating mood and behavior. Atypical antipsychotics are more effective in calming mania than the first generation of these drugs. They're also less likely to produce the abnormal Parkinson's-type rigidity or movement issues often associated with the original medications. Unfortunately, they still can trigger side effects, including:

- Blurred vision

- Drowsiness

- Dizziness

- Menstrual problems

- Rapid heartbeat

- Skin rashes

- Sun sensitivity

If you're taking an antipsychotic, your psychiatrist will want to monitor your blood regularly. Since these drugs can put you at risk for diabetes and high cholesterol by causing significant weight gain, your clinician will track your glucose and lipid levels. Also, in very rare instances, long-term atypical antipsychotic drug use can result in *tardive dyskinesia,* a condition marked by repetitive involuntary facial and body movements, such as rapid blinking, lip smacking, toe tapping, and torso contortions. Tardive dyskinesia can be triggered by other problems, but if you exhibit the symptoms, you need to report them immediately. Your psychiatrist will use many tests, including a blood count, to get a diagnosis. He or she also may monitor you as a matter of course to see that your body movements are normal.

Atypical antipsychotics are sold under several brand names based on their unique formulations. They include:

- Abilify (aripiprazole)

- Geodan (ziprasidone)

- Risperdal (risperidone)

- Seroquel (quetiapine)

- Zyprexa (olanzapine)

Atypical antipsychotics are usually taken orally several times a day. Abilify and Zyprexa are also available in injectable forms, which are administered deep into the muscle to quickly relieve the agitation associated with an urgent manic or mixed episode.

Antidepressants

Your psychiatrist may or may not prescribe an antidepressant. Even if you're prone to depressive symptoms, there's increasing evidence that these drugs can have a boomerang effect with your bipolar. How so? By balancing the natural chemicals in your brain (neurotransmitters such as serotonin, norepinephrine, and dopamine), antidepressants do a bang-up job of lifting your moods and emotions. But in the process, they can also trigger a manic episode or destabilize you so much that your mood cycling increases.

For these reasons, psychiatrists often prescribe a mood stabilizer in addition to the antidepressant. But the message is mixed on combining them, too. At least one large-scale study funded by the National Institute of Mental Health (NIMH) suggests that treating depression with an anticonvulsant alone is just as effective as pairing it with an antidepressant.[1] In fact, the current emphasis in treating bipolar depression is on optimizing your dosage of mood stabilizer with the hope of stopping the cycling and depressive episodes entirely.

If your doctor orders an antidepressant, you're likely to experience mild temporary side effects, depending on the type of drug you're getting. Fortunately today's popular *SSRIs* (*selective serotonin reuptake inhibitors*) and *SNRIs* (*selective norepinephrine reuptake inhibitors*) produce milder side effects than previous antidepressant classes. Those symptoms include:

- Agitation (feeling jittery)

- Bladder problems

- Blurred vision

- Constipation

- Dry mouth

- Headache

- Nausea

- Sleeplessness

- Sexual problems

If your psychiatrist orders an antidepressant, the two of you will want to monitor your moods very carefully for any signs that you're headed for mania.

Antidepressants are sold under several brand names based on their unique formulations. Those that are often prescribed for bipolar include:

- Paxil (paroxetine)

- Prozac (fluoxetine)

- Wellbutrin (buproprion)

- Zoloft (sertraline)

- Symbyax (a combination of the antipsychotic olanzapine and the antidepressant fluoxetine)

Antidepressants are taken orally once or several times a day

Collaboration Results in Success

The goal of treatment in general, and medications in particular, is to stop the dramatic shifts in your moods, reduce the number of bipolar episodes, block any rapid re-cycling you might be experiencing, help you function at high levels between episodes, prevent self-injury and suicide, and avoid the need for hospitalization. If that sounds like a tall order, it is, but with today's treatment options, you have a fighting chance of accomplishing your goals. You'll need to work closely with your psychiatrist, since finding the right bipolar drug or drug combination can be tricky. Keeping a daily chart of your mood symptoms, sleep patterns, and life events can be very helpful in giving your physician the necessary clues to modify your regimen. But being informed about the options up front is also important. For the most up-to-date drug information, visit the FDA's website at **www.fda.gov/drugs** or consult the NIMH's medication booklet (available at: **http://www.nimh.nih .gov/health/publications/mental-health-medications/index.shtml**).

You not only want to come armed with facts to each appointment, but also speak up and ask questions, such as:

— *"What are these medications going to do for me?"* You want the basics about the prescriptions your doctor is writing. Will they calm your moods, prevent rapid re-cycling, diminish the chance of a psychotic break, or just bring welcome, balanced relief to mind and body? Ask your doctor to explain what each medication is doing inside your brain so that it makes sense to take it. Also, make sure you understand the potential interactions with other drugs, bipolar or otherwise. If you're prone to depression, you'll want to know why your psychiatrist is prescribing an antidepressant in addition to a mood stabilizer, or just letting a mood stabilizer do the work. Don't be afraid to ask for as much information as possible. To be forewarned is to be forearmed.

— *"How long will it take to find a medication that works for me?"* Your doctor may suggest combining drugs for maximum and even synergistic effect. The old adage "Patience is a virtue" definitely applies, since it will take some time to arrive at the right "cocktail" or combination at the right dosages. Since everyone is different, your psychiatrist will take into consideration a variety of factors—your age, weight, bipolar type, symptoms, thinking patterns, and overall health—in making choices.

If you've already been through a bipolar crisis, you know that the initial therapy often involves stabilizing an individual to control symptoms. Finding the best long-term treatment plan usually takes longer, with you and your doctor working together. This is where trial and error, patience, and persistence come into play. During the next weeks and months, your doctor will monitor you to see if each drug is working and if you're tolerating it well. The reassuring news is that the closer you get to the right mix, the more likely that your side effects will improve as you do!

In my own case, it took two years before we found a combination that worked for me. Once my doctor landed on the proper regimen, my irrationality, phobias, and dramatic mood swings turned to rational, balanced, and clear thinking. Today I'm on 250 milligrams of the anticonvulsant Depakote three times a day, along with 5 milligrams of the antipsychotic Zyprexa once a day. I see my psychiatrist once or twice a year, during which time we look at my liver levels and overall health to see how I'm doing. Although the medications have been adjusted several times in the past, the dosages have stayed the same in recent years.

— **"What are the potential side effects?"** It's good to know what you might be experiencing so that you're not afraid the first time a minor side effect surfaces, and you know when to report something to your doctor that could be a major event. Even though bipolar drugs can affect just about every system of your body, fortunately many of the side effects are just annoyances. Sometimes they even lessen the longer you're on a drug that fits you. But since they come with the territory, you'll have to live with them. Your doctor can help you develop strategies to accommodate the side effects that pertain to you. I've learned, for instance, that to stay hydrated I need to drink 8 to 12 glasses of water or fruit juices a day, especially when it's hot or I'm exercising. I stay away from not only caffeine but also alcohol, since both can dehydrate. Liquor has the added "bonus" of being downright dangerous when combined with drugs, so it's definitely a no-no in my lifestyle. To stave off hunger but control my weight, I snack frequently on low-fat, low-sugar, and high-fiber snacks such as fresh fruits and vegetables. To ward off fatigue, I keep as close to my sleep schedule as possible and exercise regularly.

— **"What about herbal medicines and other alternative treatments? Can I take them, and do they help?"** The short answer to these questions is no, but it's a little more complicated than that. Doctors don't know for sure how some ancient remedies work on bipolar disorder, since there haven't been enough studies to prove that they're both safe and effective. *Saint-John's-wort,* for instance, may be a popular over-the-counter remedy for depression, but there's no evidence to suggest that it's as effective as current authorized medications in dealing with symptoms. In fact, it can interact dangerously with drugs for many conditions, including your depression. It may even trigger mania.

Likewise, a tongue twister of an amino acid supplement called *S-adenosyl-L-methionine* (SAMe) appears to help brain function related to depression. Yet, its role in bipolar disorder is not clear. It can also trigger mania. And although *omega-3 fatty acids* may help brain function in general, and even depression linked to bipolar disorder, further study is needed to quantify any mental health benefits linked to this supplement. If you're thinking of taking an herbal supplement, talk to your doctor. The goal of your treatment is to get the most out of your prescriptions. A product that sounds good on its label may actually be dangerous to your overall health or bipolar progress. Ask first so that you're not in harm's way later.

— **"Is acupuncture helpful?"** More studies are needed to determine if the ancient practice of inserting and manipulating tiny needles into the skin at specific pressure points can actually relieve depression as much as it seems to relieve pain. Based on a traditional Chinese medicine concept, acupuncture brings healing to specific organs by correcting *qi,* the body's energy flow. Although the practice won't hurt you or interfere with your other bipolar therapies, it isn't a substitute for well-documented medical therapies and should never be used as such.

— **"Should I get pregnant while using my medication?"** If you're pregnant or thinking of becoming pregnant, you need to talk to both your psychiatrist and obstetrician. Managing bipolar through a pregnancy requires balancing many risks and benefits to yourself and your fetus. Although some studies have shown that women who discontinue their medications have increased risk for a manic or depressive episode, others suggest that even if you stay on your meds, pregnancy and delivery put you at higher risk for developing symptoms. If that's not confusing enough, still other research links some bipolar drugs to first-trimester fetal problems, such as heart and neural-tube defects.

The information doctors have about the nexus between pregnancy and drug treatment is still evolving. In the meantime, your physician can help you evaluate your own situation, including the possibility of changing medication if necessary. Keep in mind that many women continue their treatment and still have beautiful, healthy babies. In weighing the benefits, risks, and consequences of your options, you and your doctors will determine what's right for you!

— **"How long will I be taking these drugs?"** It's scary to think about being on a medication for a lifetime when you consider the potential side effects. The good news is that most people don't suffer all of them, let alone the most serious ones, especially after they hit on the right drug combination. Federal law mandates that pharmaceutical companies list the hazards of taking their products. Good medicine requires that your doctor warn you about what you *might* expect. But you, too, have a vested interest in knowing and voicing your treatment concerns. Ask your psychiatrist if he or she has other patients who don't take medication. How has it worked for them? Find out what would happen if you stopped your meds on a dime or even tapered off. Will the symptoms return or get worse? You want to get a realistic lay of the land. In my own life, I've learned that being on medication and having the few side effects I deal with daily is better than living permanently in a psychiatric facility, which is where I'd otherwise be headed. Many of my clients would agree!

— **"What happens if I feel better?"** Today's bipolar drugs can work so well that many of us are duped into thinking we can abandon treatment once we feel normal. Doing so is not a terrific strategy, nor is it advisable to stop cold turkey because you *don't* like how you feel on a particular therapy. If you halt your medication, you not only miss the benefits it provides, but you also risk relapsing. Before you make any decisions, talk to your doctor. Even if the combination is making you feel lousy, there's a good chance your psychiatrist can change the dosage or find other options.

After three years in therapy and on medication, Rita stopped both parts of her treatment plan. She didn't warn anyone, including me; I was working with her at the time. Rita had been making significant progress and was in a very healthy place until she left therapy. She was productive and had a job and friends. A few weeks after her last appointment, however, her father called, frantic about her behavior. Rita had barricaded herself in her room for five days. She finally emerged, so deeply depressed that she was cutting her body.

I referred them to the hospital for immediate psychiatric care. Rita was forced to go back on her medications. Once she stabilized, however, she resumed her therapy. She told me later that she was just tired of taking the drugs and actually missed the mania. After losing her job and harming herself, Rita understood that she had to stay on her regimen or there would be relapses. She knew that trying this stunt again would put her at further risk. Rita regained her footing, and found another job and a boyfriend. This person I had worked with after the cutting incident was medicated and happy again.

I can't stress enough the importance of staying on your medications and the dangers of going off them. Unfortunately, for those of us who live with bipolar, there are no other options than lifelong treatment. In the absence of a cure, the best hope we have of normalcy is to find the right drug cocktail and stick with it.

One Final Note

Bipolar is a chronic illness for which there is no cure. It requires lifelong treatment, even during those times when you're feeling better. Unfortunately, the pharmacology connected to bipolar disorder can be overwhelming. You have to not only find the right combination of drugs, but also deal with potentially debilitating side effects.

In addition to the medications listed in this chapter, your doctor may suggest other therapies, depending on your ancillary problems or your mood state. For instance, *benzodiazepines* are fast-acting sedatives that work within minutes to an hour to relieve the anxiety and agitation of a crisis. Because they can be highly addictive, however, they're only a short-term solution before other drugs kick in. Similarly, *calcium channel blockers,* drugs normally used to treat heart problems, also have mood-stabilizing properties, although they're less effective than traditional medications. Yet they're sometimes ordered if you can't tolerate lithium or another anticonvulsant.

Although today's bipolar drugs are far from perfect, they're the reason many of us lead normal, productive lives. Hopefully in the future, medications will improve so much that we won't need trial-and-error experimentation to find a powerful option. Until then, it's important that you stay on your maintenance program, keep a journal tracking your symptoms, and be vigilant.

Here's one final point that's worth repeating: The drugs for bipolar won't rob you of your genius or turn you into a creative zombie. With the right prescription you can still be a sensitive writer, artist, or otherwise great thinker. You can be a fabulous employee or a great boss. In fact, your drug regimen should sustain and even enhance your productivity. If your medications are hindering you in any way, then talk to your doctor about an adjustment. Otherwise, they should help you to creatively, but safely, soar!

●　　●　　●

CHAPTER SIX

LIFE TOOLS

THERAPY WILL HELP you tackle many of the emotional issues connected to your bipolar disorder. Meeting with a professional, however, is only part of the process. Your work needs to continue outside the office if you're to maintain a vibrant and healthy outlook. It's critical to arm yourself with strategies that complement your sessions and keep you moving forward. You want to live confidently every day of the week, not just when you've come from therapy.

The tactics or life tools that I use consistently have kept me positive and balanced for more than a decade. I retrain my mind and change my *emotional channel* to see the world in a positive light. I use powerful affirmations to feel good about myself. I keep a journal every day to clear my head. And I set goals so that I'm always striving for the future. These tools help me release my negative emotions, alter my thinking, and keep me pointed in positive directions.

As bipolar individuals, we not only aim to put our mania and depressive episodes in check, but also to take care of the emotional issues we've stored for a lifetime. Simple, direct, and easy to implement, these tools are a practical adjunct to your therapy sessions. By doing them faithfully, they can produce results for you, too!

Retraining Your Mind

The mind is a powerful force. Positive thoughts can fuel your hopes, turn your dreams into reality, and facilitate your desire to feel love. Negative thoughts do just the opposite. They can be destructive and self-defeating, and undermine your progress.

Unfortunately, it's easy to wallow in negativity when you're battling a mental illness. You probably wonder every day why you're being constantly tested. When you're handling life's challenges through the prism of bipolar, it's natural to ask, "Why has so much adversity come my way?" Indeed, failing at a goal, being rejected by a lover, or losing someone close to you is a big enough challenge for anyone, but even more so when you're trying to juggle that with your symptoms. You're primed for anger, confusion, and other self-defeating thoughts.

But pessimism only interferes with your capacity to control your illness and otherwise function. It can make every simple task difficult. Many of my bipolar clients complain that they're overwhelmed and incapable of controlling their negative thoughts. I know their fears. When I was first diagnosed with bipolar disorder, I had no control over my emotions. My brain was constantly in overdrive from worrying, planning, thinking, and working too much. My brain darted all over the place. I'd vacillate between feeling elated and being depressed. I slept very little, which made the mania worse. Today I see the destructiveness clearly. If I had realized earlier just how much my thoughts and actions were hurting me, I could have avoided several severe bipolar episodes.

I maintain that we all have the power to train our hearts and minds to be positive, rather than negative, so that we experience the world in a new, brighter light. We do it with the words we choose, the images we create, and the thoughts we allow to enter our heads.

We do it by following in the footsteps of successful people who are accomplished at training their minds. Business leaders move forward despite a poor economy. Teachers help students excel in the face of budget cuts and their jobs being at risk. Athletes believe they're going to win even if they're losing in the last minutes of play. In fact, they've learned to concentrate so hard on the task at hand that they're *in the zone,* so to speak, once they're in the game. Fifty thousand fans could be heckling or booing their team, but they stay focused on whatever it takes to win. They have self-control.

As bipolar sufferers, we need to have the same discipline if we're to be optimistic, not pessimistic. Training your mind involves committing to change and routinely making choices. Too often, when we face the anxieties of life—health concerns, overdue bills, problems with family members, or issues at work—we default to the same self-defeating rhetoric that has stymied us in the past: "What if something goes wrong?" "What will I do?" "How can I handle it?"

By focusing on the what-ifs of life, our primary thoughts are bound to become negative. We're so beset by worry that our bodies are in constant stress. I've heard patients say things like the following: "My mom died at 52, so I will, too," "My dad has diabetes, so I'm going to have it, too," and "The doctor says I have three months to live, so I'll be dead in three months." (Say it enough, and it might just become reality!)

If that's you, you can either accept the self-talk that says you're *too sick, too old,* or *too unhappy,* or create a new reality. Perhaps you'll dare to believe that your health is getting better, that 60 is the new 40, and that happiness is just around the corner. Small changes in your thinking can mean big results in your behavior. When you learn to control your thoughts, you also make handling adversity a much simpler task.

When the father of one of my young clients faced cancer, she convinced herself that her mother would soon follow suit. She even thought her mom would die. The idea was so ingrained in her head that she couldn't get beyond it, even though there was no evidence that her mother was sick, much less terminal. We worked hard at changing my client's thoughts by having her repeat, "My mom is healthy. I will have her for many years." It eventually took. She retrained her thinking to accept that her mother would be okay, which she was.

Whatever the day brings, you can deal with it effectively by surrounding yourself with positive reinforcements from the start of the day. Read inspirational messages. Listen to life-affirming tapes. Be selective in the websites you surf. Load beautiful screen savers that suggest serenity. Throughout the day, make sure that you immerse yourself in activities and objects that bring you joy and pride. It may not be as simple as it sounds, but you can create an environment that is conducive to healing and handling anything.

The point is that you want to shield yourself as much as you can from life's everyday barbs. When the car in front of me stops short, forcing me to slam on the brakes, I no longer feel anxious or upset. I just take a deep breath and determine that a bad driver isn't going to ruin my day. Similarly, when the stock market crashes 400 points, I don't fret nervously over the money I might have lost. I just think, *What goes down today will be back up tomorrow. It's only a temporary setback on paper.*

Whatever mini or major crisis surfaces, by creating a buffer around yourself, you'll be in a much better emotional and mental place to handle it. Even if a bill collector calls or the bank notifies you that the mortgage payment is past due, the situation doesn't have to overwhelm you. If I get bad news, I take another deep breath and tell myself, *This is a piece of paper. The contents are only as important as I make them. I choose to feel good and make today positive.* Then I get busy instead of focusing on the negative. Of course, neither you nor I can ignore life's interruptions, especially if they involve our medical, legal, or financial affairs. There can be consequences if we don't respond. But we control how everything affects us. Will it be positive or negative? We choose!

Changing Your Emotional Channel

We also have the ability to create our own sense of serenity and peace by closing our eyes and playing a new movie reel in our minds. After my abduction, I worried constantly that I'd be taken again. Each time I saw a car pull up, I was certain someone would jump out and grab me. Of course, there was no reason to be concerned, but I was overwhelmed with anxiety. My therapist taught me how to visualize a place where I felt happy and safe. It was a small baseball stadium in Fort Lauderdale, Florida, where I had watched my beloved Yankees in spring training. I remembered the warm air, the clapping of the fans, and the sound of bats smacking fastballs as players raced the bases. I learned to close my eyes and snap a mental picture of that setting. I smelled the grass and felt the sun on my face. Whenever I saw a car coming and felt frightened or upset, I clicked the channel by shutting my eyes and playing the scene over and over. Thirty years later, I still use this technique to calm and relax me when I'm under siege.

You can have the same positive experience by identifying a place where you've felt happy and safe. Perhaps it's a beach, park, or favorite family-vacation spot. Just close your eyes and take a mental snapshot. What does it look like? What sounds do you hear? How does it make you feel? Once the image is set, come back to it. It's important to practice in a quiet place at first so that the picture is ingrained in your psyche and you actually feel the emotions connected to the scene. Then, whenever you're scared, angry, overwhelmed, or even insecure, close your eyes and change the channel to your peaceful place. The quicker you replace your fears with serenity and peace, the faster you'll feel better.

You'll likely have countless opportunities to change your emotional channel. Life is full of challenges, both big and small. I meet many people who want quick fixes and instant results. But it doesn't work that way for most things, especially a chronic illness. You need to change your frame of reference in a concerted way to produce lasting positive outcomes.

I'm reminded of the parable about two men who travel to the same new city. When the first man arrives at the entrance gate, he asks the guard, "Are the people here well-behaved and nice?"

The guard smiles and asks in return, "What was it like where you lived before?"

The man says, "I hated it. People were mean. They were always rude, jealous, and disrespectful."

The guard replies, "I'm sorry, but the people will be the same in this village." The man frowns, picks up his bags, and walks away.

A few minutes later, the second man arrives at the gate. He also asks the guard what the people are like in the city. The keeper responds with the same question, "What was it like where you came from?"

This time the new visitor answers affirmatively, "Everyone is so fun, kind, and supportive of each other. They're awesome."

The guard responds, "It will be the same here." The man walks into the village smiling ear to ear.

What's the moral of the story if you're bipolar? By focusing on thoughts and techniques that move you forward, your illness won't hold you back. You, too, will be smiling!

The Power of Affirmations

What you say about yourself *to* yourself can change your world. Positive self-talk is a critical step in changing your emotional channel. Too often, we let our insecurities and faults define us, rather than shine a light on all of our pluses. When I begin working with clients, they often speak of what they *don't* like, rather than what they *do* like, about themselves: They're boring. They've gained too much weight. They have too few friends.

It's true that you have to accept yourself for who you are. Being able to acknowledge your faults is a positive step. (Nobody comes into or leaves this world perfect!) But you also need to recognize your strong suits and then balance both. It takes practice to overcome your struggles and feel good about your life. But it's great when you can look in the mirror and say, "I'm beautiful, funny, and fantastic." It's awesome when you can acknowledge every day, "I've been through so much, and I'm still standing. I'm willing to fight and win all the battles of my life." It's fantastic when you no longer fear changes but can repeat confidently, "I will see more positive than negative. I will allow the light into my heart and mind so that I can shine brightly."

When you say such simple phrases—whether you call them affirmations or mantras—you're creating a powerful moment of truth for yourself. You're acknowledging that you're ready for healing, health, and happiness. Acceptance allows you to close the door on the darkness and begin to see just how bright your life will be.

Getting started is as simple as writing down five attributes about yourself that you really admire. Every morning, when you awake, say them out loud:

- "I am smart."

- "I am funny."

- "I have a great mouth."

- "I am an awesome dad."

- "I am a terrific writer."

Make sure you repeat each affirmation with *oomph* and excitement. It isn't enough to just mouth the words; you need to show some passion. Look in the mirror and be proud that the person looking back has all of those positive qualities.

If you're having difficulty identifying qualities, just think of the multiple ways your light shines every day. Perhaps you're a great colleague, co-worker, classmate, or friend. Maybe you're the best-ever husband, wife, parent, brother, sister, uncle, or aunt. Perchance you have beautiful legs, a great smile, or a face that could grace a magazine cover. Whatever you find in your personal inventory, you'll likely have many more affirmations than just the obligatory five. I can already think of others: smart, loyal, disciplined, creative, unique, and otherwise multitalented. Make your pick.

Every day I tell myself, "I feel wonderful. I feel terrific. I feel healthy." I've been doing these mantras for years. In the beginning it seemed like a waste of time. I didn't believe what I was saying, because I didn't feel that way. If I was sick, it didn't seem accurate to say, "I feel healthy." With practice, however, I actually came to believe the words. Even when I caught a stomach virus recently, I focused on feeling good and telling myself I was healthy. My symptoms seemed to diminish. The mantras became my truth. They had changed how I felt.

Repeating the mantras may feel unnatural at first. Your mind may even try to negate positive thoughts: *I don't feel happy. I feel frustrated.* But remember you've trained your brain to be pessimistic. You'll have to muster discipline and practice to make it believe otherwise. Like athletes, you learn best when you practice things over and over again. So bring on the repetition.

I've worked with clients who still have to be persuaded that they can change their thinking by talking to themselves. One young man was convinced that his diagnosis of bipolar meant he was "crazy." He thought he would never finish high school, which was an important goal. Although he was reluctant at first, I worked with him until he finally agreed to repeat, "I am mentally healthy. I am going to finish school and be happy." Of course, he had to put actions with words, but after several months of repeating the mantras, he saw that his mental health was improving, and he was fully engaged in school. My client had learned the power of selecting helpful over harmful self-talk. He had chosen the positive. It was working.

Indeed, there's a payoff for harnessing good thoughts. When you like yourself, others want to be around you. We've all watched what happens when someone with great confidence walks into a room. People are attracted to that person's aura. They respond to someone who exudes such joy. You can build the same self-esteem. By taking the high road, paved with positive affirmations, rather than the low road, littered with negative thoughts and doubts, you can exude confidence, too.

Putting Pen to Paper

Venting your emotions privately is one of the most effective techniques available to let go of your pain. Words are powerful. Keeping a diary or journal is a simple, universal way to chronicle the ups and downs of living with bipolar disorder and reconciling what it means to your life.

Clients sometimes doubt the value of writing down their thoughts, feelings, and observations. I admit that it can be a time-consuming hassle in an already-busy day. But a journal stands as a testament to your life. It serves as a repository of what you've been through and a reminder of just how far your treatment has taken you.

If keeping a diary seems daunting, start slowly. Spend just a few minutes writing down random thoughts until you get into the habit and want to add more. By reserving a set time daily, you're creating a safe space for yourself and your inner thoughts. You can yell and curse. You can rail at your disease. You can verbally "punch out" your worst enemy. You can write about anything on your mind: good, bad, or indifferent.

Your entries might not be directly related to bipolar but may focus on other challenges in your life. One of my clients found that her journal was a great way to deal with her past abuses as a child. Every time she thought about the horrendous experiences, she'd write down her feelings or draw pictures of the pain. We'd then talk through the entries so that she could better cope with them. Another woman found the exercise incredibly helpful in recording her daughter's nasty and demeaning behavior. Through our looking at her entries together, I reassured her that she wasn't at fault. She could sort out the issues and possible next steps.

Your journal doesn't have to be filled with negative material alone. It can be a reservoir for your jokes, funny stories, drawings, poems, rhymes, and even rap lines. It can document your adventures or the first inklings of your dreams and goals. Whatever it contains, you needn't share it with your parents, friends, or even your most ardent advocates. In fact, if you're a supporter of someone with bipolar, please encourage that individual to write prodigiously but privately. Confirm that you understand the need for complete freedom of expression. You won't censor or judge, because you won't look!

Since you know that the content is just between *you* and *you,* promise yourself that you'll be honest in what you write. Your journal can have far-reaching value in that it helps you reclaim important events later on. Some you may not want to remember, while others are both meaningful and helpful. One day you may even want to share your diary with your grandchildren, or leave it to future generations so that they can learn what it means to overcome bipolar disorder.

I began journaling when I was placed in my first psychiatric hospital. It was a favorite part of my day. I wrote about being medicated, depressed, and locked away. I made observations about the other young people in my same situation. I didn't believe that I was sick back then. I was in complete denial about my condition. I misplaced my early journal until several years ago when I came across it when I was moving. It was almost magical opening that relic of my history. I remembered writing in it, but seeing the words made me understand just how mentally unstable I was in those moments. I had high anxiety. I was paranoid. I was totally irrational in my thinking.

It's easy to forget what we're feeling at our most vulnerable points. But reading the actual words not only reaffirmed what I felt at a very difficult point in my life, but also gave me a sense of joy in knowing how different I am now. I can put the events of the past into perspective, knowing that I have the skills today to avoid such errors in judgment and thinking.

Many of my clients report the same experience. They say that some of their happiest moments during very hard times occur while writing in their journals. Releasing pent-up feelings on paper somehow lifts the weight of every other challenge. It gives them an opportunity to look inward, focusing on their own thoughts and observations rather than those of others. Journaling can also be a friend when you don't have many other confidants. It's very difficult to face a mental illness frightened and alone. Clearly you want all the support you can muster, but there is comfort in knowing that you can "talk" via your journal.

Those "conversations" can reveal if you're paranoid, anxious, overwhelmed, or out of control. If your writing exposes such negative thoughts, make sure you alert your therapist. These are signs that you might be approaching a mood swing or that an underlying issue needs attention. Whichever is the case, your private thoughts are relevant indicators. Don't ignore them.

At any rate, journaling is an important life tool that will help you channel pent-up energy and preserve glimpses of your past. You never know where your writing will take you. Hopefully you'll gain insight and grow. You may even pen a book about your own lessons and success!

The Power of Setting Goals

Creating a road map for your life with achievable markers or goals along the way is a powerful strategy, whether or not you have bipolar disorder. We all do our best when we're working toward something—for example, earning a degree, getting a promotion, or even starting a business. There's a sense of accomplishment and pride that the hours and "sweat equity" have paid off. But for those of us with bipolar disorder, it can help us gain better control by placing our energies on tasks, ambitions, and dreams.

In fact, goal setting isn't only about lofty long-term pursuits. It's just as important to focus on things you do daily as it is to identify what you want to achieve by age 60. The good news is that you can do both. The key is to identify specific tasks and track them closely so that you don't waver in your commitment to achieving them.

Sometimes it's difficult for people to set down objectives because it means they have to commit to them. But by targeting the things that you deem worthwhile and then following through religiously, you not only make progress with your life but also structure your time, while staying energized and positive. The first goal is to simplify the process by creating a Goals Book, a notebook or diary in which you'll list the objectives you want to accomplish today and the ones you have your eye on for the future.

Short-Term Goals

Your short-term list will contain things that you want to do right now. It may even include day-to-day responsibilities that you're already fulfilling: Take your medication and refill the prescription when necessary. Attend your therapy sessions. Shower, shave, and brush your teeth every day. I know that keeping up with basic hygiene seems like a no-brainer, but when you're stressed, sometimes it's a burden that's too heavy to bear.

When you're making the list, don't limit yourself to just one or two short-term goals, however. Every routine and important thing you do should be identified and entered. Perhaps you've committed to walk or jog four out of every seven days. Maybe you're trying to lose two pounds a week. Perhaps you want to take the first crucial steps in going back to school. Putting simple short-term steps down on paper will make even larger goals very doable. It will also add needed structure to your day.

Don't be timid in your commitment. It's easy to use phrases like "hope to" and "want to" in crafting your objectives, especially if you've never had to focus in this way. But suggesting that you *might* do something leaves too much room for *not* getting it done. You need to express yourself forcefully: "I *will* go to the gym three times this week." "I *will not* drink alcohol for the next seven days." "I *will* take my medications every day." "I *will* make plans to spend time with a friend." "I *will* finish reading Blake's book." These are clear goals that you can accomplish. At the end of the week, you'll be able to check off specifics in your Goals Book that you've committed to and completed successfully.

I also suggest identifying what you're thinking or feeling with each entry. You might write: "I wanted to go to the gym three times this week. I only went once. It's hard to push myself these days, because I'm feeling lazy and tired. Hopefully next week will be different." I'd even add the specific steps you intend to take during the next seven days to ensure that you live up to your promises. You might say something like, "Next week I will go to the gym in the morning, when I have more energy, rather than the late afternoon, when I'm often dragging." Once you've targeted your short-term goals, you're ready for the big time!

Long-Term Goals

Just as short-term goals will help structure your day, long-term ones will help structure your future. They may take time and unwavering commitment to bring to fruition, but setting, tracking, and achieving markers in your life will keep you moving forward despite your mental illness. Keeping them in your Goals Book will be particularly useful, since you might have many ups and downs, fits and starts.

We all have secret fantasies. Perhaps yours is to live and work in Paris. Or maybe it's just to find a soul mate closer to home. It's easy to put off such dreams, especially if you're struggling with a mental illness. We ignore a goal because we aren't sure we can handle the challenge of achieving it. But I believe you're able to do anything you set your mind to. I've witnessed many people with bipolar become healthy individuals who are capable of accomplishing things they once thought impossible.

Of course, a little prudence doesn't hurt. It's great to let your mind fly with all the exciting possibilities. But your goals should be ones that you have a true chance of achieving. They satisfy your interests and meet your talents, but they're also within the realm of possibility. Remember, you want to see success. If you're not technically savvy or computer literate, for instance, you're unlikely to build an Internet company from the ground up. But if you have a viable idea for an invention that relates to your job or hobby, you could make it happen. Similarly, if you have never climbed a mountain but love jogging around the city, running the Boston Marathon is probably a better goal than hiking Mount Everest.

Whatever you choose, be bold in your pronouncements and ready to own them. If you truly want to become a millionaire, for instance, state your mission forcefully. Then ask yourself, *What will it take to actually put seven figures into my bank account?* You can set down manageable, incremental goals to realize your wealth: Go back to school. Change jobs. Grow your business. Write the great American novel. Actually bring that thingamajig you've been talking about inventing to market. By brainstorming about your thoughts and fears, you're now ready to set smaller steps that will point you in the right direction.

Declaring what you want is a freeing first step, even if you're not ready to receive it today. When you write down a goal, you can look at it. You can come back to it. You can think of how to make it happen. You can break it up into doable steps that become weekly markers to accomplish your bigger objective. If, say, you want to get that thingamajig invented, the incremental steps might be:

- "I *will* find an engineer to design a prototype."

- "I *will* determine how to register a patent."

- "I *will* identify sources of financing."

- "I *will* survey companies that might buy the idea."

Obviously, there are more steps to the process, but by declaring your intentions in writing, you can begin to see the possibilities.

I worked with a young writer/photographer who was very unhappy with his career, even though he had tremendous skills, along with knowledge about his industry. For all of his talents, however, he couldn't get to the next professional level, let alone find his specialty publication niche. We worked diligently on honing his focus and establishing goals for identifying potential employers, sending out résumés, and making follow-up phone calls. Within two months my client found a dream job at a nature magazine. Once he started the process, he saw the possibilities and went after them. Eventually, his goal setting paid off big-time.

Similarly, when a second client wanted to start a party-planning business, she was overwhelmed by all the organizational tasks involved in a start-up. I had her break them down into incremental steps or goals that she could meet in a reasonable time frame. The further my client got into the process, the more energized she became about the possibilities. She realized that by setting and meeting goals, she also was moving closer to her ultimate objective: being her own boss. Eventually, my client was not just dreaming about a business; she was running it. Today she's in demand as a high-end creative-events guru. Her clients include both corporations and private individuals who are willing to pay top dollar for her special touch!

Establishing and tracking long-term goals can cast light on your future in a way that you haven't experienced in the past. It can help you sort out your greatest ambitions and make sure you work toward them. Just as you identify the roadblocks preventing you from achieving your short-term targets, you can do the same introspection with taller agendas.

Also, remember that goals can evolve. As human beings, we have an organic ebb and flow to our lives. As an adult you likely don't have the same ambitions you did as a teenager. There are probably more important things in your sights today than buying an Xbox or finding a date for the school dance. (Okay, you still might want the Xbox.) And maybe some of the long-term dreams you're chasing now germinated when you were a youngster. Perhaps you've always wanted to be a doctor, lawyer, or firefighter.

As a boy I was certain I'd be the next Don Mattingly. I was confident I could follow in the footsteps of the famed New York Yankees' first baseman—that is, until reality sank in. My aspirations exceeded my skills, which weren't destined to match his by any stretch of the imagination. Fortunately, I had other doable ambitions. It was when I was hospitalized at age 15 that I first thought about writing a book on my experiences with bipolar disorder. At the time it seemed like a joke, especially since some medical professionals had deemed my life over. Seventeen years later I accomplished what I set out to do. I was persistent and never gave up. Today I'm proud to say that Hay House has published the book you're reading. I'm glad people didn't puncture my dreams! Now I have a new goal: turn this book into a bestseller!

The point is that you'll likely add, change, replace, and even eliminate specific objectives as you achieve or rethink what's important in your life. The key is to make progress. Setting and meeting goals is one step in your march toward success. I encourage you to salute yourself and the work you've been doing already. Be happy in making even small gains. They will lead to larger success. With short- and long-term goals in place, you'll accomplish more than you could ever have imagined for your life.

One Final Note

Controlling your bipolar disorder is fundamental to having a successful, happy life. It's amazing the good you can do for yourself if you routinely vent your feelings, change your emotional channel, applaud what you see in the mirror, and set goals for your future. By taking a few simple steps every day to reinforce your positives, you can grow by leaps and bounds. Of course, it will take time and effort. Nothing improves by just wishing it so. But when you invest in training your mind, you'll see a difference in how you feel. Much like switching the television or radio dial to find a better program, turning your emotional channel can create a better you.

●　●　●

PART III

CEMENTING RELATIONSHIPS, BOTH OLD AND NEW

CHAPTER SEVEN

HEALTHY CONNECTIONS: HOW TO HARNESS SUPPORT

IT'S IN YOUR best interest to develop a team of individuals who will support you in tackling your bipolar disorder. Forming strong bonds with others is part of being emotionally stable, especially if you're battling a mental illness. I have found that cultivating relationships with a wide variety of people can yield many benefits, not the least of which is to break the isolation of your condition.

But how do you create a quality network of individuals who can become a strong safety net, too? The good news is that there are many ways to form a circle around you. By tapping immediate and extended family members, friends, co-workers, mentors, teachers, classmates, your pastor or rabbi, and, of course, your therapist, you can create a strong ring of support.

In my own life, I've had the good fortune to be backed by a supportive family, but I've also reached out through classes and other activities to make new friends. Over the years, I've met many special individuals who have become my sounding board when I needed another perspective and my cheering squad when I deserved praise. They've been there to alert me to changes in my behavior and sometimes even keep me tethered to reality.

People with bipolar often complain that they lack friends or the capacity to make friends. Some people have been hurt so much in the past that they don't feel they can trust again. I can certainly understand your fears. I haven't walked in your shoes or confronted your particular concerns, but I know, based on my own experience in dealing with bipolar disorder and helping others deal with their illness, that your fears are real.

Yet I believe we are all capable of pursuing healthy, productive relationships. It's within our grasp. Just as there are strategies for getting through the day with your bipolar, there are strategies for getting connected. Whether that involves steps to strengthen your ties within the family or tactics for meeting people with like interests, you can create better relationships. Once you've mastered them, you'll be healthier and happier for it!

Family as Support

Family is a critical lynchpin for most of us who have bipolar. Our parents and siblings usually are first responders to our emotional ups and downs. They've been there through thick and thin for as long as we've had the diagnosis. They've witnessed the very highs and the very lows. They've even had to step in and step up.

Yet how we define *family,* especially in terms of intimate confidants, may be different from a traditional mother-father-sibling relationship. It may include an aunt, uncle, grandparent, cousin, co-worker, classmate, or friend. We may even feel closer to the people next door or the couple down the street than to our own kin.

Family is whoever offers the kindness, love, and perspective you need to gain strength and get a handle on your bipolar disorder. *Family* includes individuals who truly know and understand you. When I was sick, I fooled people all the time with my sunny disposition. They saw me as charming, passionate, and bursting with energy. But the people who knew me best—my mother, father, siblings, and friends—also knew that I wasn't healthy. They had insight about my behavior that others didn't share.

They were also loyal. I was terribly sad and frightened during each of my psychiatric hospitalizations. To be locked in a mental unit is overwhelming for anyone, most of all as a teenager. Yet each day, my parents brought me my favorite foods. I still remember my elation when my dad rolled in with a Kenny Rogers Roasters chicken dinner. I loved those meals. He wasn't the only one, however. Even when I felt like giving up, my grandparents, other relatives, and friends gave me strength, hope, and courage to comply with my treatment. They carried me with their good wishes for my restored health and complete recovery.

I know that not everyone has the same good luck with their parents. There are countless people who are dealing with their bipolar disorder without the loving and supportive relationship of the two people they should be able to trust the most. Our parents are supposed to guide us into making positive changes. It's upsetting when we don't get along, especially if they don't understand our illness or are facing demons of their own. I've worked with many clients whose mothers or fathers are alcoholics, are experiencing depression, have anger issues, or are confronting other emotional battles.

Yet when faced with the reality of emotionally distant parents or the absence of other caring relatives, these clients have constructed their own closely knit group. They've found people who are capable of listening to them, moving them forward, and even praising them on the way to success. They've discovered that others can provide the security, intimacy, and insight they've missed in the past. Maybe they don't share biological ties, but they've bonded just the same. You can have a similar positive experience. It's never too late to create a supportive family! You just need to find the missing links.

Friends and Colleagues

Lacking friends is a common issue for bipolar individuals. I've met many beautiful, creative, successful, intelligent, and dynamic people who complain that they're alone and isolated. They wish they had more people to talk to, especially about their illness.

It's hard to build friendships. It's sometimes overwhelming for people with any mental illness to let others into their lives. *Will they like me? Will they accept who I am? Am I going to be judged?*—these are common concerns that even healthy individuals have about developing relationships. Then add the overlay of a chronic mental health problem, and the next questions become: *What will my new friends think when they hear about my illness? Will they want to associate with me once they know?* You are not alone if you have such doubts. Rest assured, others have them, too!

As a bipolar individual, however, you need to have other people in your corner. Sharing with your parents is wonderful, especially if they've supported you through some pretty bleak days. Finding a therapist who will give you a professional perspective on your illness can add immeasurably to your growth. But forging relationships outside your immediate family and mental health team is also important.

The key is to find individuals who accept you as you are, support your development, and lift you up. The company you keep can play a major role in both your journey and mood. Positive people can enrich you. Pessimistic people can de-energize and frustrate you. You know the kind of person of whom I speak. When you say, "I don't know if I like my job," your friend comes back with, "You're right to wonder. Your job sucks. You don't make enough money. You're an idiot for working there, and you should quit."

True friends have your best interests at heart and want to help you in your decision making. When you express your frustration, they'll come back with questions like these: *What turns you on about the job, and what turns you off? Are there things that you and your boss could change to make it a better experience? Have you thought about applying for another position within the company?*

Obviously, there are many directions to go with such a conversation, but the important takeaway is that people who have your back will prop you up, rather than bring you down. They'll work with you to sort through issues and choices. They'll help you discover what's right for you, not what *they* think is right for you. As a therapist, life coach, and friend, I've learned that a little guidance and advice is a positive thing. We all need sounding boards. Being challenged is part of good decision making. But in the end, people do their best when they make their own choices. You want to be confident that the final decision, after you've weighed the pros and cons, is *yours*.

Finding Soul Mates

So how do you find those unique individuals who will not only earn your trust but also possibly be a soul mate? There are many ways to link with the right people. As human beings, most of us yearn to be part of a larger community. Whether it's through a church, fraternal organization, or professional group, connecting with others of like mind and spirit gives us a sense of belonging and helps build self-esteem. It can also bring out our inner light.

I know it's not always easy to put yourself out there, especially if you've been bullied, put down, or rejected in the past. Yet joining can be worth the effort. When I moved to Los Angeles, my first goal was to make new acquaintances. Since I knew few people, it was an important part of adjusting to my new home. I started by listing activities I knew I'd enjoy, and soon found people with similar interests. I even went out of my comfort zone by joining an improvisational comedy class at the famed The Groundlings Theatre and School in Los Angeles. I wanted to meet creative people. It worked.

Beyond just enjoying the experience, I tried other ways to connect with my improv group outside of class. When the school gave us tickets to see the advanced students perform in their own revue, I took it upon myself to organize an outing. Although it sounds like a small effort now, it was a risk for me back then, especially when no one responded immediately. I could have felt rejected, but I just waited, and before long I had some gracious replies. Even though many of my classmates couldn't attend, they were encouraging about my efforts. One returned the favor with an invitation to a jazz show. We went, and became fast friends. If I hadn't stepped outside my comfort zone, I never would have expanded my circle. Sometimes it takes persistence and a little courage to make lasting friendships. But you won't know until you try.

Finding Your Passion

If you don't know what makes you feel alive, then it's time to take inventory. I believe strongly that we all have talents and skills that will fulfill us, whether we do them for a living or for fun. Finding and pursuing yours can lead to many rewards, not the least of which is sharing with others. (You may even have the great fortune of turning a sleeper interest in building train sets or planning parties into a lucrative profession.)

I encourage you to identify those things that light your innermost fire. There are no right or wrong answers. The exceptions, of course, are drinking in excess, doing illicit drugs, or turning to other addictions. Such destructive forces will only bring darkness into your life and isolate you even more. Putting your energy into constructive pursuits, on the other hand, will lift you up and expand your world. By building, growing, and exploring, you'll find not only positive outlets, but also the real possibility of connecting with healthy people who are eager to take the journey with you.

Giving of Yourself

Among the lessons I've learned in life, the biggest is that giving matters. We are most connected to our inner light when we lend our hearts, energy, talents, and love to others. The ability to help is within all of us, and the need is certainly there. Throughout the world, people are hurting. It doesn't take a lot to direct our excess energies into making a difference. Donate clothes to a local charity store. Mentor a failing student.

Volunteer in a soup kitchen or senior center. Whether you're rescuing a pet, opening your home to foster children, or walking for a good cause, you can make a difference.

Working with the homeless in New York City showed me just how blessed one could be, despite battling a mental illness. Each day, I was making small but important differences in their lives by helping them find food, clothing, and shelter. In return, they showed me how to appreciate what I went home to each night: food, a house, heat, and my own bed. The basics I took for granted were luxuries to them. Yet these people never ceased to inspire me with their wisdom, kindness, and hope.

In Judaism we're called upon to do a *mitzvah,* or good deed, every day. I've enjoyed many positives from the mitzvahs I've pursued in life. You can, too, no matter what your religion, ethnicity, or age. Taking up a worthy cause or performing a daily good deed has many positive ramifications. You may meet like-minded others. But most important, when you give of yourself and focus on others, you'll feel mentally alert and emotionally connected. The effort required is a small price to pay for such big rewards.

Healthy Connections: Support Groups

Meeting other people with bipolar disorder can be very comforting. Whether you have a circle of friends or feel completely alone, there's something very reassuring in connecting with individuals who have been where you are and who know what you're facing. People feel a great sense of harmony and peace when they're among others who share similar stories. There's definitely strength in numbers.

As I mentioned in Chapter 4, it's important not to confuse a support group with group therapy. If your psychiatrist suggests the latter, you'll work jointly with others in a very structured format on specific issues related to your diagnosis. Since a psychiatrist, psychologist, marriage or family therapist, social worker, or mental health professional conducts group therapy, you get immediate feedback on your challenges and progress.

Support groups, as I touched upon previously, are often a recommended adjunct to your formal treatment. Led by volunteer peers or facilitated by professionals, these sessions are designed to help people navigate the day-to-day challenges of bipolar disorder by sharing their collective experiences. The agenda can include any topic relevant to living with a mental illness. Whether that includes venting, listening, or exchanging advice, the point is you're doing it together in a safe environment. The passion and interest of participants usually make support groups positive forces in helping you stay the course and move forward.

Although your therapist can likely put you in touch with a local group, you can also find these resources by contacting organizations such as the National Alliance on Mental Illness (**www.nami.org**) and the Depression and Bipolar Support Alliance (**www.dbsalliance.org**). Both offer wide-ranging materials, plus access to their online and person-to-person support groups and other tools.

My own informational site, the Bipolar Disorder Directory (**www .bipolardirectory.com**), also includes links to other types of support groups, ancillary to your illness. Because I'm very determined that people with our mental illness never have to face their manic depression alone, I started a second site, Will Listen (**www.willlisten.com**), several years ago. It uses the power and 24-7 availability of the Internet to connect sufferers around the world. Through our online community, people have free access to others who have honed their coping skills.

Other sites can also be helpful. The beauty of **www.meetup.com**, for instance, is that it facilitates creating, organizing, and advertising "meet-ups," or face-to-face meetings, of communities of people. Whether you're looking for a bipolar group or trying to broaden your activities in the community, Meetup is a good first stop. Just search the site by topic and zip code to see what's happening near you. You'll likely find people who share your interest not just in bipolar disorder but also in card games, dancing, or yoga. And that's just a start.

Starting Your Own Group

Is it wise to start your own bipolar support group? People with chronic illnesses are sometimes so enthused about their own progress that they're eager to share their ideas. It's terrific to want to help others cope with their bipolar disorder, but you need to make sure that *you're* healthy first. If you've only recently been diagnosed or your moods are still unstable, you still have some personal work to do. As I mentioned before, there are plenty of resources available to be an active participant in a support group. Be one!

If you've been stable for several years—that is, your therapy and meds are working beautifully—you might be ready to become a leader. I encourage you to check existing resources for training and direction. You might find a natural opening in a group that already exists. Also, don't be afraid to approach your doctor or therapist about the possibilities. They are likely connected in the mental health community and can guide you.

Having said that, starting your own support group can be a powerful experience. It can help you break through your isolation and give you a sense of purpose, especially since you're doing something for others in addition to yourself. It will take organizational skills and a commitment to providing a safe and constructive environment. But you can make it happen, either on your own or by tag-teaming with others who have the disorder and share your interest in forming a group. By combining your up-close bipolar experiences with your passion for getting better, you can make changes in your own life and those of others.

Step 1: **Identify your target audience.** Are you organizing this effort for bipolar sufferers of all ages, or just adults or just teenagers? Do you want to focus on spouses or parents and siblings of people with the disease? Or is this going to be an open forum for everyone? Targeting your audience will help narrow your agenda.

STEP 2: **Find a meeting place.** Most communities have many possible locations for self-help meetings that you can either rent or use for free: churches, libraries, senior centers, restaurants, coffeehouses. You'll likely find an open room somewhere that can accommodate your group. You'll obviously have to do some sleuthing, however. The questions you'll want to ask when you call might include:

- "Is there a fee, and if so, how much?"

- "Do we have to buy food?"

- "Do we have to be out by a certain hour?"

- "Is the room available at the same time every week?"

STEP 3: **Advertise your event.** With computer programs at your fingertips and a Kinko's in most cities, you won't have difficulty creating a quick flyer that you can distribute to local mental health professionals, schools, and other organizations. Also take advantage of the free bulletin-board functions on websites such as the aforementioned **www .meetup.com**. You can use the site to introduce and describe your group, schedule your event, and alert the public that you exist and are looking for members. Within days of listing my "meet-up" group for bipolar in the Los Angeles area, I had 40 attendees.

STEP 4: **Create a vibrant agenda.** Although prep work is important, your real target is the meeting content itself. I suggest having a fairly loose plan for each session. Let the energy take you where people need to go. You certainly can have key topics in mind. Perhaps you stimulate conversation by focusing on how the disorder has impacted everyone's lives. What can they share? Or maybe you want people to give advice for handling the symptoms. What's each person's experience? There's no one correct topic or way to handle a support group, except that you want to stay focused on issues that are germane to the disease. You don't want to detour into specific family or other matters unless there's a clear connection to the discussion.

There are many creative things you can do with a support meeting. You can even have participants teach a lesson they've learned about dealing every day with their illness. Also, any number of relevant books (including this one) would make great fodder for a group discussion, if that's where participants want to go with the agenda.

For starters, make sure you include *Call Me Anna: The Autobiography of Patty Duke* (by Patty Duke and Kenneth Turan) and *A Brilliant Madness: Living with Manic-Depressive Illness* (by Patty Duke and Gloria Hochman) on your list. Both focus on the actress's struggles with this illness. Likewise, I highly recommend anything penned by clinical psychologist and author Kay Redfield Jamison, Ph.D. As one of the foremost experts in the field—as well as a bipolar sufferer—Jamison brings her professional and personal perspectives to the forefront in *An Unquiet Mind: A Memoir of Moods and Madness*. A second book, *Touched with Fire: Manic-Depressive Illness and the Artistic Temperament,* which I mentioned earlier in this book, explores the idea that bipolar disorder tends to run in artistic or high-achieving families. Whichever of these books you choose, I'm confident that you'll find great wisdom and talking points from their messages. So get those Kindles and Nooks working!

STEP 5: **Give everyone a chance to talk.** It doesn't matter how many people are in your group. You will gain enormously from the interactions. Each time I run a session, I learn something new. Although we share a common disorder, we all bring a unique family history and perspective to the table.

I remember the first support meeting I ever conducted in California. Even though I had left it open to anyone with a bipolar connection, I wasn't sure who would show up or how the event would go. But within minutes of my welcoming speech, the room at the Laguna Beach restaurant filled with men, women, and teens who were eager to tell their stories. One man shared that his daughter had committed suicide due to her bipolar disorder. Others mentioned their troubles with dating; taking care of children; and conquering their anger, fears, and feelings of isolation. A teenager and her mother described the young girl's struggles as she tried to fit in when she felt as if she stuck out.

With each story came sympathetic nods and the realization of shared pain. It was obvious by the end of the evening that bipolar disorder, sometimes complicated by life experiences, had challenged all of us in similar ways. If there was another common thread to the evening, however, it was that we weren't alone. More than 25 of us were facing our struggles together in that Italian restaurant. Many in the group thought it worthwhile enough to stay in touch, with some of them meeting each week.

Even if it's just you and one other person sitting in the plush chairs of a Starbucks, partnering in or forming a group will give you a new outlet. In fact, a case could be made for the intimacy of having four or five people meet in your living room. Whatever the configuration, the goal should be to give everyone a few minutes to talk during each meeting. From my own experience, I can tell you that it's gratifying when other people actually listen to and support your voice. It's healthy for you both!

Uniting as One

As bipolar individuals, we have a unique opportunity. Although this condition has changed our lives, we have the chance to change the lives of many others. We can also be ambassadors for our own illness. What do I mean by that? Bipolar disorder needs a generation of heroes who will help reverse the stereotypes of this illness. Even though we no longer have to cower in the shadows or hide behind a stigma, we still need to show others that we aren't wacky, crazy, or weird. We don't have to be shuttered away in a hospital. We can live in the community.

I admit that it can be difficult to dispel old myths and negative images in seeking understanding and acceptance, especially when others with our disease are publicly unleashing their mania. The rest of us are left to clarify misconceptions and change attitudes. Yes, we *can* point to stellar examples of public figures living positively and totally in control. Thankfully, there are many of them.

Yet getting personally healthy and staying healthy is the first step in shedding light on bipolar disorder. Nothing is quite as powerful in correcting misperceptions about a chronic illness than showing friends, family, and neighbors that we're just one of them. By managing our symptoms constructively, we can be role models, ready to engage in thoughtful dialogue about our illness. The people around us don't have to fear an angry outburst or strange behavior, because they're witnessing a calm and thoughtful human being. When we communicate from a healthy, productive place, we become role models for living successfully with bipolar. If people see us as measured individuals, they're likely to open their hearts and minds to our stories. Hopefully, we'll be comfortable telling them.

Several years ago, I began my personal crusade to educate the public about bipolar disorder. I started by opening up with colleagues and friends who didn't know I had the disorder. I had constantly worried that people would learn about my condition and judge me, but no more. When I finally understood that I didn't have to be embarrassed because this was a medical issue, I didn't live in fear. I felt so healthy that I could share with anyone. Some people were shocked because I was so "normal." They wanted to know everything I felt comfortable telling them about my bipolar.

At first I was just fielding questions from the people closest to me. Then I started giving talks to local groups who were interested in the topic. I even had an opportunity to do a satellite media tour with radio personality Dr. Drew Pinsky to educate college students across the country about the importance of handling bipolar in a healthy way. In our 30 joint interviews, he spoke about the medical aspects of this disease, while I filled in the personal story. It was an amazing experience. A student called me after hearing one interview to tell me that it had saved his life. He recognized the symptoms in himself, sought a diagnosis, and got treatment. If he hadn't heard my story that day, he felt sure that he would have killed himself. Something in my story gave him the courage to go on.

Today I share my journey with members of school, business, civic, and other groups. It's been terrific to go public with a personal issue that was once so embarrassing that I didn't dare whisper it to anyone. I started the Will Listen website as a way to reach out to individuals with bipolar and their family members. The mission of the website is to provide a social community and support, either through my office or online, for people wrestling with mental illness. I don't want anyone to ever feel alone. In addition to helping bipolar individuals, I hope my efforts help raise public awareness so that attitudes change.

Ensuring Our Rights

Even though in the U.S., as people with mental illnesses, we're protected generally under the Americans with Disabilities Act, or ADA, we still need to ensure that we're able to achieve educational, work, and other opportunities. We should also think boldly in terms of strategies, legislative or otherwise, to improve our collective prospects. I'd like to see businesses, for instance, allow bipolar individuals to suggest work structures that will help them not only be productive but also reach the top of their game. Whether that means instituting a specific schedule or adjusting a job to fit someone's capabilities and skills, I believe we can create great success when we work together.

Likewise, I was fortunate enough to get accepted into college, but I believe that universities should step up their efforts to evaluate applicants with mental illnesses based on potential, not just grades and tests. Anyone who has battled bipolar in high school has likely suffered setbacks. You can certainly argue in your application essay that you underperformed because of a chronic mental illness. But how you did academically when you were first struggling with your disorder may be different from how you *could* do now that it's under control. You may have fallen short of your God-given capabilities back then. But you still have the potential to go to the top of the class now. Hopefully, the college "powers that be" will have enough foresight to give you the chance.

Finding Leaders among Us

Although we each have a personal stake in countering the negative images of our collective illness, sometimes that's not even enough. Every time a bipolar individual is involved in some heinous act, the world hears about the downside of our disorder. We need an organized effort to educate the public and disseminate the upsides of living healthily with it. Whether that means raising the profile of fabulous groups such as the DBSA, or creating an entirely new nonprofit entity, it's important that we have a central resource and voice. We certainly don't have to pioneer the concept. There are plenty of role models in other organizations that have united successfully for a common goal. For instance, the NAACP (National Association for the Advancement of Colored People) and GLAAD (Gay & Lesbian Alliance Against Defamation) have been effective in advocating for the civil rights of specific minority or disenfranchised Americans. I like to think that if we funnel the same high-level energy into defending our cause as these folks do in defending theirs, we can produce many positive results.

Also, I hope that within my lifetime, the bipolar community will be able to coalesce around a national leader much as how African Americans coalesced around the late Reverend Martin Luther King, Jr. I believe that our fortunes as a group would increase precipitously if one or more people emerged to give this mental illness a positive face in the media and a dynamic presence among lawmakers. In any case, by standing tall and together, we raise awareness. By showing courage, we become symbols of power, purpose, and hope.

Healthy Choices:
When to Share Your Bipolar Diagnosis

People often ask me when they should share the news of their bipolar. My response is that there's no magic time. The right moment is when you're comfortable and ready. The important point is that someone's reaction may not be what you expect, either positive or negative. People have differing opinions, and you might be surprised by what you hear.

For that reason, it's important that you're not just emotionally ready to open up about the details but also prepared to field the responses.

Of course, you're not going to run into school or your workplace shouting, "Hey, I have bipolar! I just spent a month in a psychiatric hospital!" You want to be circumspect and selective. As an adult, for instance, you may not even want to share your illness with others at work. After all, it's your professional home. This is where you make a living. You have to weigh the risks and benefits, just as you would with any other disease. If your bipolar is under control, there may be no reason to alert others, unless you're comfortable sharing with your colleagues and co-workers or they truly need to know.

Theoretically, bipolar sufferers in the U.S. are part of a protected worker class under the previously mentioned federal ADA, a wide-ranging civil rights law that prohibits discrimination based solely on either mental or physical limitations. Under the 1990 legislation and its 2008 amendments, you can't be fired or denied promotion simply because you have a health issue. (There are exceptions, of course.) Instead, you may be able to negotiate what's called "reasonable accommodations"—things like shortened work hours, job modifications, or even extended absences—due to your illness. (For specific information about your situation and the law, you can call the U.S. Department of Justice ADA Information Line, 1-800-514-0301, or visit **www.ada.gov**.)

Even with the ADA hovering above, the risk of opening up about your diagnosis or asking for any favors from your boss or colleagues, however, is that people will know about your illness. The benefit is that if they do, they may be supportive and impressed by how you juggle work and a chronic illness. In either case, you want to be a productive colleague, willing to get the most out of your job and contribute at the highest-possible level. The Depression and Bipolar Support Alliance has published a wonderful guide, *Wellness at Work,* which will help you navigate the workplace (**www.dbsalliance.org/pdfs/work.pdf**). I encourage you to check it out.

Teen Strategies

If you're a teenager facing bipolar, you'll have your own set of challenges, in some ways not very different from those of an adult. Finding acceptance can be scary at any age but particularly during adolescence. At school, it can be hell trying to survive the petty criticisms of other students, whether or not you have a mental illness. If you're bipolar, however, you have the additional fear that you might be treated differently, if not ignored. I know. I've been there. I was popular and confident before my diagnosis. I wasn't afraid to approach or talk to someone I didn't know. But when I became sick, I lost my courage—not forever but for a very long time. I was nervous and shy. I was constantly worried that people would somehow find out that I was bipolar and think of me as weird. It took a great deal of therapy and work to rebuild my self-esteem. I found, however, that you don't lose those old connections.

After I left the hospital, two of my best friends, Dane and Jeff, made it their business to hang out with me. They treated me no differently than they had before the diagnosis, banishing any notions that people would turn away from me once they knew I was bipolar. They were warm and funny. They kept me smiling, even though I felt overwhelmed at times. They not only stood by me at a critical point in my healing, but also promised they would be there for me whenever I was ready to go back to school. They were good at keeping their word. They gave me the courage to set aside my anger and to rebuild other friendships. Because of them, I had hope that life could go on.

Whatever your age, letting people know that you're bipolar can be a relief for both of you. While you're no longer in hiding, your friend or co-worker will know that if you exhibit any odd behavior, there's a medical reason for it. When you're finally ready to share, explain the condition, offer to answer any questions, and encourage them to read further. Also, ask them to be honest with you, especially about your behavior. Often the people around us can see a shift in our moods first, even when we're blind to it. Your friends may be the best barometers you have for detecting an approaching manic or depressive storm. Use them.

Whatever the timing of your disclosure, the good news about admitting to having a mental illness is that you can be yourself. You also can be honest about the restrictions on your life in dealing with a mental illness. Most of us with bipolar are on medications, so we have to curb our drinking, get plenty of sleep, and stay away from negative influences like street drugs. When those closest to you know that you're being treated for a mental illness, they'll likely understand and respect your choices. Telling my first girlfriend and other friends that I was bipolar was freeing. I could be myself without worrying that someone would see my medications and discover my secret. Once it was in the open, I felt tremendous relief. I had worried about sharing my story. My friends, however, didn't flinch when hearing it.

Thank You!

· ·

It's painful to have bipolar disorder. It's also painful to watch someone struggle with it. Whether you're a parent, sibling, spouse, or close friend, if you're an advocate, you're likely to feel frustrated, overwhelmed, confused, and even scared on occasion by the potential of this disorder. Among my own therapy clients, I routinely saw family members who were in great distress over what they were witnessing. It's extremely difficult to support loved ones who deny that they have a major mental illness, refuse to get help, or are working through their issues. That can be a ton of grief for anyone!

But your continued emotional support is vital. You're helping enormously when you urge a loved one with bipolar to see a mental health professional. You're a true advocate when you track that person's symptoms, setbacks, and progress, and let him or her know your observations. You're a lifesaver when you recognize that this individual is in deep pain and needs immediate help.

You contribute by just being patient and persistent. It may take some time for your loved one to come to grips with the possibility of a mental illness, accept it, and undergo treatment. The journey to full health is not easy with this disease. Like addicts and alcoholics who fail repeatedly before becoming sober, we, too, have setbacks on the road to success. We may endure several manic or depressive episodes before asking for help. We're likely to be angry, stubborn, and test your patience in every way. You will, no doubt, be frustrated and turned off many times.

But please don't give up. As someone who has benefited from the enormous largesse of family and friends in dealing with my own mood disorder, I will tell you that your continued participation is key in overcoming this illness. It's often the deciding factor in keeping a bipolar sufferer in therapy. It's sometimes crucial in stopping a person from self-inflicting pain.

During my initial episodes, I, too, refused treatment. I had no insight about my illness. I didn't believe anything anyone around me said either. I thought I knew best. It took a great deal of time for me to understand the dangers of being bipolar. Remember, I was that 15-year-old boy running around Manhattan trying to be the first "pilot" to fly without an airplane. It's easy to see why my family was so frightened. My thinking had veered way off course. I had such poor judgment that I could have died. (Good thing I never found a "runway" from which to take off, or my landing would have been ugly!) It took several hospitalizations and medications for me to see that treatment worked!

I survived those turbulent times, because deep inside I knew that I was loved. People cared about me. I might have given up if it weren't for friends and family who rallied in my defense. They demonstrated in so many large and small ways just how far they were willing to go and just how much they were willing to do to help me get well. They had infinite patience. Once I opened my eyes to the reality of my illness, I could see the pain *they* were experiencing in watching me deal with it. Even during my darkest days, I wanted to stick with my treatment and rebuild my life, because so many people around me kept me moving forward.

If you've ever doubted your role as an advocate, please don't. You're making enormous, even lifesaving, contributions. When we work together as sufferers and supporters, we have the potential to create healing and hope. You deserve applause and a major thank-you for doing your part. *Thank you!*

. . . .

One Final Note

As all of us who live with bipolar disorder understand, navigating the road to recovery can be fraught with many obstacles. Having a mental illness can be isolating and emotionally traumatic. You're likely to feel alone at various points in your journey, particularly when you're first grappling with the diagnosis. Developing a support network of individuals who understand and accept that you have a real disease with real symptoms that need real attention is of paramount importance in moving forward. The people around you can make all the difference in the world to your emotional stability and physical well-being.

Of course, you're responsible for what goes on in your own life, but there's no shame in involving others. In fact, the further you reach, the more possibilities you'll have for enriching yourself. Since each person brings unique skills, talents, and experiences to the table, it's to your advantage to be open and accepting of others. Your illness doesn't have to be the focal point for each interaction, but having people in your life whose opinions you value and trust is worth gold. They can help keep you stabilized, and move you forward. Trust me; I know. I've benefited from a wide circle of family, friends, and fellow bipolar patients. They've either walked in my shoes because they have the same mental illness or beside me because they care that much. I wish the same good fortunes for you!

●   ●   ●

CHAPTER EIGHT

LETTING LOVE IN

LETTING LOVE INTO your life takes work, energy, and determination. Millions struggle with finding appropriate partners, dating the right people, growing relationships, and keeping marriages intact. When you have bipolar disorder, it's easy to worry that you'll never find the love of your life or that the love of your life can't deal with your diagnosis.

I completely understand. I've had those fears, too. But I've also been blessed with a wonderful wife, so I know that it's not only possible to share yourself with someone in a healthy, romantic, and seriously committed relationship—it's probable. The opportunities exist. Unfortunately, many of us sabotage ourselves before we get started. We don't take care of past hurts or current issues before venturing into the dating world. When we try, we fail. When we fail once, we give up completely. Or we don't even try, because we don't know how to proceed.

So what arrows do you need in your quiver to achieve love? As with everything else, the strategies for finding and nursing a healthy romantic relationship start with your own emotional health. I had to appreciate myself, rid my thoughts of past hurts, and be bold in my pursuit to live my romantic dreams. When you're filled with positivity and joy, you can attract that special someone. Trust me. Jen is my proof.

Finding Love: Strategies for Success

You attract love by loving yourself first. It's as simple as that. Once you're content in your own skin, the world will open to you. You'll win friends and find lovers. There's a reason why confident people achieve relationships. When someone exudes a positive, open aura, others are more inclined to approach. Aren't you drawn to individuals who appear comfortable in their own skin?

Most of us would say yes. We like it when someone engages us in conversation, shows an interest in what we do, or just makes us feel good about ourselves. When people know and accept themselves, they're ready to draw others into their sphere. And you can become that open, confident, giving person by looking inward and reaching out.

STEP 1:
Accept That You're Bipolar

Like many people, you have a chronic illness that needs lifelong treatment. Unfortunately, many of us are so preoccupied with our mental illness that we don't see ourselves as the beautiful human beings we are, with or without our condition. We wallow in defeatist thoughts, convinced that we don't deserve better: *I am not lovable. My depressions and manias will be too much for anyone to handle. I've tried for years but will never find a relationship.* It's tough to identify love when you're constantly worried. But you can't let your bipolar mask your other qualities and strengths. You have to change those negative thoughts into positive affirmations: *I am lovable. My mania and depression won't get in the way because they're under control. I will find someone whom I love and who loves me.* You deserve a terrific and loving relationship with someone who makes you smile, encourages you to do well, and brings out your best.

Prior to my diagnosis, I was fearless about asking girls out. If I was attracted to someone, I didn't think twice about it. I was confident and outgoing. But five psychiatric hospitalizations took their toll. When you're struggling to survive or live between home and a mental institution, it's easy to feel worthless and emotionally spent. I felt like a wounded bird that couldn't fly. I didn't know if others would accept me. Why should they? At that point I didn't accept myself. I was overwhelmed with the fear that girls wouldn't share their hearts with me, because they saw my illness as some sort of plague.

My therapist helped me accept the very real fact that none of us is immune to problems. We all have struggles. Millions of people face mental and physical illnesses, addictions, and loss. It's part of the human experience. I wasn't the only person living with pain or grappling with a challenge while trying to have a productive life. Other people certainly face situations that dwarf mine.

I also realized that I had the capacity to smile, have fun, make people laugh, and even help others feel alive. I could add value to those around me by being a great listener and an enthusiastic doer. I could even inspire people to have hope and be happy. Those qualities, my therapist assured me, would be beneficial when I was ready to date or have a serious relationship. I also came to accept that my mental illness was in check and was unlikely to be a determining factor in the outcome of my life.

Step 2:
Forgive the Past

It doesn't matter where you are in your love life, you won't find a healthy relationship unless you've tackled your indiscretions, guilt, and anger. Others may have hurt you. Perhaps a spouse, friend, family member, or co-worker broke your trust, treated you badly, or walked out when you really needed someone in your corner. It's easy to let the actions of an individual take away your confidence and make you feel like less of a person.

For example, it took a long time for Jay, one of my clients, to admit that his insecurities about dating were directly related to the merciless put-downs he was subjected to as a child. Even his family members got into the act. Once he finally came to grips with the hurt, he could start rebuilding his confidence. Jay eventually accepted himself as an attractive, lovable guy who deserved a great relationship. In time, he met a wonderful woman, fell in love, and got married. He's no longer the lonely man I first met and helped. Jay and his wife now have a beautiful family.

In my own case, I had more than just insecurities linked to my bipolar to address before I could start dating. I was also suffering the aftermath of my parents' nasty divorce. I was scared that I'd have the same type of relationship experience as my mother and father had. Fortunately, I learned over time that my path in life would likely be very different from their paths. I was my own person. My choices would be mine alone. In the end they were just that.

Yet you pay a huge price when you give someone else that kind of control. You lose the joy of new relationships and the possibility of meeting your soul mate. Remember, you didn't deserve the harsh treatment, but you also shouldn't harbor the hurt. Whether you're trying to achieve a healthy relationship or improve a not-so-healthy one, you need to forgive your past mistakes and those of others. The more quickly you deal with the destruction, the more quickly you'll be whole and in harmony with the world. You'll also be open to partners who actively support your happiness and growth.

STEP 3:
Accept Your Reflection

You've taken a gigantic step when you can stand in front of a mirror and admire the face and body you see. Maybe your nose is crooked or your ears are big. Yet if we were all supermodels with camera-friendly features, none of us would be special and unique. Right? Instead your specific look sets you apart from others, unless, of course, you have an identical twin. When you stop focusing on your flaws and start appreciating your features, you see your face—and maybe even the world—in a different, positive light.

If I take my shirt off and look in the mirror these days, I don't see that I'm too heavy or out-of-shape, or that I have this fault or that defect (all of which may be true!). I see someone who's handsome, strong, and an all-around beautiful guy. I proudly tell my reflection, "You are a good person. You make a positive difference in the world. You are proud to be *you*." When I accept myself, I'm happily ready to take on the day.

You don't have to be perfect to be successful at life *or* love. We can all learn from my former client, Marjorie, who never let her full-figured frame get in the way of dating. She seemed to be a magnet for great guys. She also put herself in situations where she would meet men who appreciated her plus size. At one point, Marjorie belonged to a group that sponsored dances and events for larger people. Partygoers flocked to them. When you accept and position yourself for love, you can find it. You *can* succeed. There is someone who will appreciate you for *you*.

Step 4:
Be Confident That You're Capable of Loving and Being Loved

I know it's difficult sometimes to accept affection from others, but we have it in our hearts to give and receive love. In fact, you're probably already demonstrating your capacity for connecting with your heart. You show love when you wrap your arms around your grandmother in a big bear hug. You show love when you commit acts of kindness and caring for total strangers. No, they may not generate the same butterflies-in-your-stomach sensations we associate with attraction and that special someone. But love comes in many forms. Every time a gardener nurses a seedling into a flower or a teacher nurses a young intellect, he or she shows love. Even if you're stressed by the challenges of your mental illness, you've likely extended yourself in ways that we can define as *love*. Now you just need to open your heart to the wonderful experience that comes with loving—and being loved by—a boyfriend or girlfriend, partner or spouse.

STEP 5:
Make Connections

Whether you're looking for a casual partner or trying to find the love of your life, you won't make progress unless you're willing to connect with new people. Whatever your fears, you need to be out and about. If you love playing sports or attending the symphony, join a league or volunteer as an usher. Similarly, if you're religious, join a church, synagogue, or other place of worship. You'll not only experience the spiritual rewards and peace of an active faith, but you may even find someone with real possibilities who shares your beliefs.

Whatever you do, commit yourself to make love happen. When I was rebuilding my life, I knew that having a girlfriend was an important part of it. I wasn't ready immediately to ask someone for a date, so I started honing my confidence by strengthening my friendships. I needed to know that I could be comfortable just relating to people. I also worked very closely with my therapist on healing.

Eventually, I pushed myself into social situations where I'd meet girls. It helped greatly that they not only were nice to me, but also viewed me as a regular guy. When I did share about my illness, they didn't think of me as sick or damaged. I had been healthy for over a year when I met Stacey. By then I was in college and ready to venture into a girlfriend-boyfriend relationship. From day one, I wanted to tell her about being bipolar and the serious issues I had faced previously. My better instincts, however, told me to hold off on sharing the news until Stacey got to know me as a stable individual. After three months, our relationship had become serious enough that I wanted to tell her. I was very nervous as I explained the facts: "I have bipolar disorder. I was hospitalized with serious problems in the past, but I'm healthy now. I'll have to take medications for the rest of my life to treat my illness."

The good news is that she was gracious and understanding. To say that I was greatly relieved when she didn't bolt might be the biggest understatement of my life. We continued dating for a long time before finally going our separate ways. Yet we maintain a friendship. I will always appreciate her accepting me. It had a major impact on my ability to overcome the stigma of bipolar.

I can't guarantee that everyone will be like Stacey, and stick with you or be there for you if you have bipolar disorder. No one can make such predictions. What I know for certain, however, is that there are many terrific people in our world. You can find individuals who will accept you, befriend you, and treat you as an equal human being. I hope you find people who have learned that all of us have value, especially those of us with a mental illness.

Surfing for Love

Should you use the Internet to connect with potential friends and love interests? There are definite positives to social networking, even though you need to be cautious anytime you rely on clicking a mouse rather than shaking a hand to make your connections. Tapping the web for contacts can widen your potential circle by giving you access to individuals all over the world. It can help build your confidence and social cues by letting you interact before you physically meet someone. Addresses such as **www.not4dating.com** or **www.badoo.com** can be great places to link with new friends who share your other interests.

But here's a word to the wise, especially if you're turning to a website for a dating prospect or life partner: whenever and however you engage in social networking, be careful about what and how much you share at first. Being discreet is always a good policy, especially when you're feeling your way with someone new. Also be a little leery of what this person says about him- or herself until you have a chance to follow up. If you decide to finally connect in person, make sure you follow all precautions: meet in a public place, and let someone know what you're doing and where you're going. A face-to-face encounter will help you evaluate someone's body language, voice intonations, or other personality quirks and cues. It gives your intuition, those inner instincts that usually kick in when we meet people, a chance to work. You can finally look the person in the eye and assess what you see, think, and feel. So keep your antennae up. Once you put a live face to an e-mail name, it's time to trust *and* verify.

. . . .

Open Your Heart and Take a Risk

You can have all the self-esteem in the world, but at some point, as the old saying goes, you'll have to fish or cut bait. You need to harness your confidence and move beyond your fears.

When I was thinking of proposing to Jen, I was nervous about making such a big commitment. Even though I had worked through many of my issues with a therapist, I was still conflicted about my parents' divorce and the residual hurt from a former lover's cheating. But then serendipity stepped in. I submitted my story to the *Dr. Phil* show, because the producers were looking for relationship tales. To my surprise, the show chose mine. Before I knew it, I was flying to California from my then residence in New York City. When I arrived at the airport, a cameraman recorded my every move as I was ushered to a taxicab. When the "driver" turned his head, much to my amazement I was looking at Dr. Phil McGraw. He greeted me with, "I hear you're nervous about popping the question." We were off.

At dinner with him that evening, I recounted my past experiences with cheating partners and my fears that my marriage would end in divorce like my parents'. He reminded me that it wasn't fair to blame Jen for someone else's sins. She couldn't change my past. She could only affect my present and future. Plus our relationship was very healthy, especially when compared to the many problems in my parents' marriage. Dr. Phil encouraged me to search my soul about my feelings. I realized how much I loved Jen and wanted to spend my life with her.

Once we decided I should propose on the show, we used a ruse to get Jen from New York to California. I lured her with the suggestion that I had a potential opportunity to sell a documentary I had produced about foster children to a Paramount division. I just "happened" to get

VIP seats to Dr. Phil's show, since it's taped at Paramount's Hollywood studios. It wasn't a hard sell, since Jen is an avid fan. She thought she was just going to be an audience member until the show's spotlight turned on us. I gathered the courage I had tucked inside for so long, and popped *the* question. Of course she accepted. It was an amazingly beautiful experience.

I couldn't have done it had I not learned a valuable lesson along the way: never let individuals who hurt you in the past take away your opportunities or destroy your hope and dreams. If I had done that, look what I would have missed.

Keeping Love: Strategies for Success

It would be great if partners didn't have tempers and relationships didn't take effort. There'd be nothing but kumbaya in the world. But since we're all human, we're unlikely to skate through life without worrying about what our partners think, do, want, or say. Even those of us who have terrific mental health still have our moments, moods, and *meshugas*. Whether you describe your problems in English or Yiddish, they still have to be addressed. When there's stress between the two of you:

— **Make sure your anger is directed at the right source.** People with bipolar often take out their agitations, frustrations, and confusion on the people closest to them, when they're really mad about something else. If someone has truly hurt you by his or her words or actions, you certainly have the right to be mad. But be clear about what's really going on internally before you react.

— **Limit the fighting.** If you become angry, sometimes the best thing to do is to step away. Since arguments can escalate quickly once someone's fuse is lit, you might want to work preemptively by avoiding topics that stoke the flames. If you do wade into uncomfortable waters, slow the action by removing yourself. Taking a walk will not only defuse the situation, but also limit the damage that usually occurs when you say or do something out of anger. Since you can't take it back, it's better to calm down first.

— **Consult the professionals.** If you really believe your relationship is at risk, see a counselor. Someone who's trained in helping people work through issues calmly and clearly can also help you communicate in a more measured, constructive way. You'll likely be asked to listen while your partner speaks and then acknowledge what he or she has said during the session. Don't worry. You'll have your opportunity to vent, too, since this approach relies on equal time for everyone. Couples therapy can not only save your relationship, but also teach you how to get your needs met without resorting to fisticuffs.

— **Unleash the tension.** There are ways to let out your feelings without creating long-term damage to yourself or another person. If you truly need to vent, you also need to remove yourself from the situation and direct your frustrations elsewhere. Scream in your car or the woods. Hit a punching bag until you're physically spent. Anything you do to release pent-up tension and negative energy that doesn't put others at risk is a positive step. Your therapist or coach also has techniques to help you discharge your feelings. If you are absent a professional's help, talk to a trusted friend who has calmed you in the past. You need a strategy for handling your outbursts so that you're not verbally or physically laying a hand on anyone.

— **Live and let go.** You can't change or erase the past. If your current partner has cheated, or hurt you in some other way, you can't undo what this person has done. You can only make one of several choices: let the hurt fester, forgive and work together on a positive relationship, or leave. Whatever course you ultimately take, the first step will be to decide if the marriage or partnership is worth keeping. If it is, you and your mate have work to do in identifying any underlying problems and building new trust. Whether or not you decide to remain connected, don't hold on to the negativity. It's not healthy or constructive to stay angry, especially if you want to find someone new. It will only sour you to potential suitors.

— **Make your relationship meaningful and fun.** Your partner is supposed to be your best friend, the one person in the world who accepts you for all of your flaws, and supports you in every way. You need to treat this person as a deserving and integral part of your life. Sadly, many of us, with or without bipolar disorder, behave very badly toward our mates. We yell at them. We put them down. We make their lives generally miserable. This is not the recipe for a healthy marriage or relationship. If you want a partnership that flourishes over time, you need to treat your mate with the same respect that you want in return. Smile more. Yell less. Think of every little thing you can do each day to make your partner feel appreciated, wanted, and special. You have many hurdles to overcome with bipolar disorder. You don't want your mate to feel as if the fight isn't worth it. It's your job to lift up this person. By showing that you truly care, you'll both be healthier for it.

One of the ways I knew that Jen was the woman for me was that our relationship wasn't a struggle. It flowed easily from day one. Fortunately, we have the same positive dynamic today, even though we still disagree now and again. We work out our issues by talking them through. We also commit daily to our marriage. These are the same building blocks that I recommend to others. You can't expect a relationship to flourish unless you're willing to work on it.

Bipolar Times Two

Setting ground rules is important in any partnership. Yet when both of you suffer a mental illness, doing so is even more critical for extending the love. Being a good spouse or lover is not rocket science. (Nor is it just about great sex!) It's showing that, despite bipolar or another chronic illness, you're capable of pulling your own weight in a healthy, committed union. Coming together over two mental illnesses gives new meaning to the vow "in sickness and in health." Whether you're sharing your life with an emotionally healthy or similarly challenged individual, you need to work for a win-win situation. Here are some steps to take:

— **Manage your own illness.** Vowing to stick with your treatment plan and live healthy is as important for your relationship as any other promise you make before God, family, and friends. You have a responsibility to yourself first to take your medications, see your therapist, attend your support group, and pursue any other avenues to keep balance in your life. But you owe it to your partner to keep yourself in recovery. It's a vow that you should be willing to take.

— **Encourage your partner to stick with treatment.** If you're involved with someone who has a mental illness, it's imperative that you support and encourage this person in his or her own growth. Relationships can crumble due to many pressures. Yet when either of you refuses to come to grips with a chronic disease, the results can be disastrous for you both. It's tough enough to take care of yourself if *you're* not well. It's worse yet if your partner is also unstable or even extremely volatile. The two of you can do tremendous emotional and physical damage by just being together. But if you're committed to your own recovery and that of your partner, you help your relationship immeasurably when you stay the course and lend support.

— **Agree to monitor each other's symptoms.** Because you and your partner have a vested interest in ensuring continued recovery, it's important to track each other's behavior. The plus of pairing with someone who shares your mental illness is that your soul mate understands what it's like to be bipolar, and won't judge you. The other bonus should be that you have a teammate who is interested in both your mental and physical health, and capable of eyeing a change in your conduct. If you or your partner spots any shift in the other person's mood or behavior, you owe it to the relationship to tell it like it is.

— **Share responsibilities and assign household tasks.** The activities of daily living can be daunting when you're chronically ill. You have to not only worry about taking care of your health, but also accomplishing ordinary chores. Someone still has to take out the garbage, clean the house, and care for the kids. Managing adult responsibilities when you have a mood disorder can trigger overwhelming pressure. Distributing the work systematically can ease that strain, however (a good strategy no matter who is your partner!). Although Jen isn't bipolar, we've divided our household tasks so that neither of us is unduly stressed. For instance, she's an early riser, so she cares for our daughter, Tyler, in the morning, while I take over later in the day. Since Jen's great at shopping and I'm good with finances, we divvy those responsibilities in a pretty traditional way. Our goal is to keep our house running smoothly by sharing tasks and operating as an organized team.

— **Keep up your end of the bargain and cover each other.** You and your partner owe it to each other to step up to the plate. Relationships can easily go south when one individual feels that the other isn't doing his or her fair share. As challenging as it may seem, keeping your illness under control is only one part of the bargain. You each need to carry your weight in your partnership and house. Also, recognize that when one of you can't function normally, the other may have to double up on tasks. It doesn't matter which of you is slipping into an episode or experiencing some other sickness. As a significant other, you or your soul mate must provide cover. If neither of you is doing well, you'll need to rely on your therapist and support system more than ever.

— **Get advice from your counselor.** The input of your mental health professional is important for many issues involving your bipolar disorder. Marriage or a committed relationship may be among the most important. Your therapist can help you sort through the challenges. Whatever you two bring to the table, you need the tools to create a vibrant relationship that has the chance to succeed, despite your collective illness. It doesn't serve *either* of you for *both* of you to be habitually unstable. Even if it feels comfortable in some weird-dependency sort of way, it isn't a healthy choice. Your therapist can help you avoid those pitfalls while building a strong future.

— **Communicate your needs.** Letting your partner know your desires concerning intimacy and sex is essential. Developing quality relationships is all about being truthful and open, especially when it comes to the most private areas of your life. You need to feel free and safe to make requests, call for compromises, or say anything you please about what you like or don't like. It doesn't matter which one of you wants sex every day or prefers to wait until the weekends, talking through your intimacy issues is the only way to arrive at compromise. The same can be said about any part of your life, romantic or otherwise. The best relationships occur when two people are confident that they're supported, loved, and *heard*.

Letting Go: Strategies for Moving On

None of us wants to be rejected. It can be jarringly painful. Still, it's the potential price you pay for taking a chance at love. We're all vulnerable when we let down our guard and open ourselves to intimacy. If you have bipolar disorder, you have the additional challenge of hoping that the illness won't be a reason for losing love. In the interest of full disclosure, you never want to hide a legitimate medical issue, especially a mental illness. It's not fair to you or the other person. But the reality is that sometimes a boyfriend or girlfriend will not understand your disorder and will prefer to move on to someone else. That's just the way of life.

I used to be upset if a relationship didn't work out or someone I really liked didn't share my ardent feelings. I grew to realize, however, that each liaison was an enormous learning experience. I was becoming more secure in my ability to love and care about someone. I was also preparing myself to find the woman I would eventually marry. With each lost love, I evaluated what I learned from the relationship and what I then knew I wanted in a long-term partner.

By the time I met Jen, I had whittled down the qualities to a select list. I had also put the drama and pain of my failed romances completely behind me. My happiness was in knowing that I finally had found my ideal mate. It had taken years to believe in myself and find the courage to give my heart to someone else. But sharing my life with her was worth the effort and risk. I didn't have to look further. I knew deep inside that she was *the one.*

Even if your spouse is well aware of your condition, there are no guarantees of a lasting marriage. I've worked with couples who were at a crossroads because one partner could no longer deal with the other partner's disease. Despite talking through the issues, the nonbipolar partner simply wants to move on. As painful as a broken relationship is, you deserve someone who can commit to you and living with your disorder. If your mate can't be persuaded otherwise, you may have to let go, too. It might be a relief for you both. It can even open doors for you to move on.

Domestic Abuse: Strategies for Survival

If you're a battered partner or spouse, you need to get help immediately. You have a right as a human being to live in a safe environment without the threat of physical, mental, or verbal abuse. I know that battered women, in particular, stay in abusive relationships because they think they're too weak to move on. I also know that it's not easy to make life changes, especially if you have financial concerns and you're saddled with a mental illness. But for your own good and that of your children, admit that the abuse is occurring, and seek counseling. There's no shame in wanting help for your bipolar disorder. There's no shame in wanting help for this issue either.

If your partner refuses to address the problem or make changes, you have no other choice than to get out. Staying in a toxic relationship and environment will put you at physical or emotional risk. Most communities have resources to help battered individuals move on with their lives. If nothing else, tell your therapist, doctor, or priest that you need help, possibly even a safe house.

It's difficult enough to handle a mental illness, but adding violence to the mix only compromises your progress toward a healthier you. At the least, abuse is unacceptable behavior. At worst, it's a crime. Besides leaving you with potential life-threatening injuries, it will further zap your energy, darken your outlook, and snuff out what's left of your inner light. Harnessing your strength to deal with it, however, is a giant step toward healing your life.

One Final Note

You *can* experience love. Having bipolar disorder does not disqualify you from a healthy romantic relationship. You have the power to open your heart to other people. If you do, you'll be richer for it. Showing and giving love can brighten your life and enrich you in many gratifying ways, not the least of which is newfound intimacy. When you like yourself, accept your faults, and boldly pursue your objective, you might be surprised by where your bravery will take you, by how far your loving arms can reach. Perhaps you'll find a new friendship that turns into a dating relationship. Maybe you'll lasso a genuine love interest or even the love of your life. Whatever the outcome, by paying attention to affairs of the heart, you can enrich your mind, body, and soul. Your bipolar disorder doesn't have to restrict you. Love can blossom for you, too!

•   •   •

PART IV

MAPPING A NEW LIFE

CHAPTER NINE

PERSISTENCE AND THE POWER OF HOPE AND SOUL

I KNOW THAT it's easy to give up when times are tough. It's tiring to face each day knowing that you have a mental illness. You want a quick resolution for issues that have been with you for years and maybe even decades. But now is when you need to harness your tenacity and tap your inner strength. Your psychiatrist can give you the right medication. Your therapist can walk you through your issues. But only you can demonstrate the determination to get, and stick, with the program. That might be a frightening concept, given the challenges you've already faced and the insecurities you might feel. But I promise, you have it in you to do what you need to do to overcome this illness.

If you need an example of the good things that can happen when you're put to the test and stick with the mission, think of what it's like to be a U.S. presidential candidate. The process can test someone's mettle like few other pursuits. People who chase the dream subject themselves to the most grueling primary and general-election schedules imaginable. They undergo enormous scrutiny as they battle fellow candidates and their critics. Yet they persevere, even though they don't know if they'll win or lose in the end. In the meantime, however, the candidates worth their salt also sharpen their messages, strengthen their skills, and connect clearly on their positions. The person who survives that gauntlet usually has met the challenge and kept a great attitude. The one who ultimately wins the voters shows incredible inner resolve.

Controlling your bipolar is a race that you *must* win. You'll need to pull together all of your assets, both external and internal. It will require the best of what you have to offer to yourself and those cheering you on from the sidelines. Mental health professionals can give you the tools, but you'll need patience, hope, and your inner self working in tandem to help you pull off a win. But I have faith in you! You may not feel it at the moment, but you are an awesome individual, not only for running the race, but also for crossing the finish line!

Patience Is a Virtue

Among the many tools to fight your bipolar disorder, you'll need patience above all. Sadly, we live in a society where taking time is not necessarily a virtue. People want quick resolution on problems that they've been dealing with for years. But that's when you need to harness everything you've got inside.

Changing inner beliefs and patterns can take months, if not years. I remember when I was trying to lose weight. I'd work out several hours a day, seven days a week. Two of my meals each day consisted of just salad with no dressing. Not surprisingly, I lost 30 pounds in one month. Sure I looked great and, yes, I enjoyed hearing my friends comment on my new svelte frame. But I hadn't learned how to eat healthily yet. Food was still my drug of choice to battle stress and pain. Once I hit my goal, I returned to my old habits. Voilà, my weight skyrocketed again. I had to learn how my emotional issues were linked to my eating habits. It took some time, but once I caught on, I was on my way to the healthy weight I maintain to this day. I finally realized that being the tortoise with weight loss actually produces better results than being the hare.

Perhaps you need to learn the same lesson with your bipolar. You, your therapist, and your physician will have to work together over time to make the kind of progress that you likely want overnight. Taking small steps over weeks, if not months and years, is the only way you can control a chronic illness. The longer you're engaged in the process, the better the success. Slow and steady definitely wins the bipolar race.

Tapping Your Inner You

We live in exciting times in terms of treating bipolar disorder. There are many tangible steps you can take to control your symptoms: accepting medication, undergoing therapy, joining a support group. Together they make for a formidable strategy. But I believe two other *intangibles* are also necessary in driving and directing your recovery. Even though scientists may find them hard to quantify, both play a critical role in strengthening your inner resolve.

Hope

I've known many pessimistic people, clients and otherwise, who have said to me, "Why should I have hope for my future when my life is going downhill? Nothing good ever happens to me." If you have that attitude, you probably can't expect too much. When you're caught up in your own tough circumstances, you're never going to experience the joy of living. Negativity hurts the quality of your life and the lives of others. When the weight of the world is parked squarely on your shoulders, you're not able to move freely. You're not able to love. You're not able to support the people supporting you. Bitterness, especially about your bipolar disorder, is like riding a wooden horse. You're going nowhere.

Hope, on the other hand, can help you change the course of your disease. It allows you to press forward, make plans, and even overcome obstacles in your path. You can do anything you set your mind to when you trust that there will be a better day, that you'll achieve normalcy, and that you can have a future. It doesn't mean you won't have obstacles and doubts. But by seeing the world through the lens of hope, you face your mental illness and other adversities with confidence in what the future holds.

Several years ago I made a conscious decision to focus only on those things that would support my positive, hopeful attitude. Instead of listening to the news, for instance, I'd watch uplifting videos or read motivational books. As such, I love to listen to Houston mega-church pastor Joel Osteen. I'm not a Christian, but I appreciate the powerful message he preaches every Sunday from his Lakewood Church. It centers on a common theme of faith and hope. He talks of how God can change our lives instantly for the better. He's mentioned how his mother never gave up after hearing that she had cancer. She could have said, "It's over." But she soldiered on and has been cancer-free for many years.

Even when our life on Earth is ending, many of us have faith in an even happier existence on the other side. Whether or not you share such spiritual beliefs, hope can help you handle the direst of circumstances. Because I have hope, I'm able to keep much of the negativity of my past in the past. I often say that my mental illness is the best thing that ever happened to me. Why? It changed me.

Not only have I learned how to control my thinking, but also my illness has made me a more sensitive, creative, and even intuitive person. My wife hears a song on the radio and quickly determines if she likes or doesn't like the melody. I, however, hear every vocal intonation and background acoustic. I'm in tune with the meaning of the lyrics, the pain in the singer's voice, and the emotional content of the message. Intense, yes, but I can't help but experience the sounds and sights of life with great fervor. I believe that a key to my newfound sensitivity is that I now see the world in terms of great hope. I'm willing to take chances.

Wherever you are in your journey, hope can sustain you through the bad times and push you toward the better times. It can put you in unison with the higher universe or just help you achieve your highest calling on Earth. *Hope*—it's a simple four-letter word with profound potential. When you have bipolar disorder, having *hope* in your quiver can help you shoot for the stars. Just ask me. I know!

Soul

Singer Billy Joel pretty much sums up life in his song "All About Soul." Through years of battling bipolar disorder, I've learned that how we deal with a mental illness is driven, in large part, by who we are inside. Whether we define *soul* in terms of a spiritual or religious belief, or simply a mystical concept, it's the moral or emotional essence guiding our lives. For whatever reason, having a soul separates human beings from other living creatures. I can't explain the whys and wherefores, but I believe that your soul drives everything you think, believe, act on, or say. It's that inner voice we call a *conscience* and that inner sense we refer to as *intuition*. Some of us aren't so good at listening to it. We discount it, refute it, or try to turn it off when we don't like what it says.

But those of us who are guided in life by that inner essence have an ever-present confidant to teach us lessons, offer us insight, and direct us to do the right thing. How does it work? Sit silently for a minute and ask yourself something pressing. Perhaps the question is, *Should I take this new job?* Although your mind will generate an answer based on salary, growth potential, and other objective indicators, your inner voice or soul will be your gut check. It will help you cut through the fears and hesitations to make a decision that follows your heart.

Your soul not only helps steer you toward the best choices, but also fuels your inner light. When your mind and body are in harmony with your inner you, you'll have the quiet sense that you're doing right by yourself. When we recognize, rely on, and live up to our inner voice, we shine.

In everything I do, I hope my actions reflect the real me. I choose not to be depressed, angry, or confused when life hands me a situation, because I want my inner light to glow. Before the Jewish holidays, I was picking up a few groceries. Before I got to the supermarket, I asked Jen if she would please transfer some funds among our accounts so that I could pay for groceries. Thirty minutes later I was in the store, buying flowers for her and delicacies for our celebration. I was in a good mood, chatting with my fellow shoppers and just enjoying the experience—that is, until I tried to use my bank card to pay for the items. It was denied. I called my wife and calmly asked her if she had made the transfer.

She apologized and said she had forgotten but would do it immediately. After ten minutes, I called again, and she assured me that she had made the deposit. Even after two additional attempts, however, the transaction was still denied.

I was embarrassed but refused to lose my calm. I just put the cart aside, went to the bank, and withdrew the funds, which had finally been credited to the correct account. Within a few minutes, I had my groceries. Many people would have arrived home in a huff and started an argument over the mix-up. But I saw it as a personal teaching moment. I was learning patience at the same time that I was behaving in accordance with my soul. I was quietly in control.

When we pursue behaviors that put us in harmony with our inner light, we're no longer just propelled by impulse to act or make decisions. In matters of life and bipolar disorder, we're guided by wisdom and our deepest, truest voice: our soul.

Rules for Survivors

It's a challenge to juggle all the things you need to juggle in recovery. There's no question that your life is different in many ways from the lives of people who are unencumbered by a mental illness. You have concerns that will never cross their minds, just as they have concerns that may never enter your head. Hopefully, once you've become comfortable with your diagnosis and treatment, you'll be able to accommodate your new routine with relative ease.

It's my wish that you'll learn with time that patience is your friend and that hope really does spring eternal. You have a future. I pray that you'll also make choices that are in sync with your inner voice. Whatever course your recovery takes, there are absolutes that should guide you. Tuck these rules in your mind or even fasten them to your refrigerator with a magnet. They may keep you focused on the ultimate prize, your good health and sanity.

RULE 1: **Recognize that bipolar is a long journey.** You must accept the fact that it will take time to change your mind and behavior. I know that it's sometimes difficult—in an age of instant messaging, overnight fixes, fast food, and five-day cures—to grasp the long-haul investment of controlling a chronic condition. But overcoming any health issue or other trauma requires commitment and patience.

Jen had a magically close relationship with her mother, Randy. They were best friends who talked every day. Randy was even the first person to meet our daughter, Tyler, the moment after Jen and I witnessed her birth. So it was particularly difficult for both of us when we learned that Randy was dying of chronic obstructive pulmonary disorder at age 61. Randy had been a smoker with other health issues, so in some ways it wasn't a surprise when we got the call that she was rapidly deteriorating in the hospital.

We raced to Florida to be with her in her final days. As my mother-in-law struggled to stay with us, Jen spent every waking moment holding her hand and telling her how much she meant to us. When the doctors finally removed Randy's breathing tube, my wife felt almost unimaginable pain. To this day, Jen is still healing. She could have let this loss consume her in many negative ways. Instead, she's working through her grief by attending therapy and reading positive materials. She, too, finds great comfort in her family and friends. She's also willing to give herself time.

There's no magic bullet for mending Jen's broken heart, any more than there's a magic bullet for mending bipolar disorder. They both can exact a mighty toll. The lesson to be learned, however, is that we decide how we deal with life's ordinary and extraordinary traumas. The choices we make either destroy us or make us stronger.

RULE 2: **Be honest in your treatment.** Since your success with both medications and therapy is dependent solely on where you are at a given point in time, you need to make sure that your mental health professionals have an accurate picture of your current status. With bipolar disorder, it's never a good thing to hide how you're thinking or feeling. You need to say what's on your mind.

Rule 3: **Forgive yourself.** As painful as your foibles feel, you need to accept them and make changes. If your past behavior hangs around your neck like a weight, you can't possibly pick yourself up and move on. None of us can rewrite the past. We only have the power to improve the future. This *is* the first day of the rest of your life. Use it well!

Rule 4: **Love yourself.** When you really care about your well-being, you begin to make better choices than you have in the past. That includes sticking with treatment; adopting healthy-lifestyle choices; and getting rid of any habits that could be harmful, such as smoking, drinking, and using drugs. Also, stop putting yourself down. You can't love yourself if don't like what you see in the mirror. Love the shoes you're in (or the *socks,* if you don't have the shoes!).

Rule 5: **Forgive others.** You aren't the only person who suffers from pent-up anger toward those who have wronged you. Even if you're in the right, holding court against someone who's hurt you in the past won't give you any satisfaction. Believe me, I've tried it, and it doesn't work. You only gain power when you let go of the pain and angst over people and events that have harmed you in the past. When you can say, "I forgive you for your insensitive and cruel behavior," you are freed to move on. Trust me, it's better to let go!

Rule 6: **Accept that everything happens for a reason.** Neither you nor I wanted bipolar disorder. But there's a reason that it happened to us. I believe a divine force guides all of us at each moment. We are where we're supposed to be, doing what we're supposed to do. You can't redo your life, but you can redirect it. By accepting your mental illness, you're poised to grow in beautiful and abundant ways. I know. I never could have imagined on my worst days that I'd be healthy and strong. But once I trusted that I could make good choices, I was headed for the positive life I have today.

RULE 7: **Appreciate that the future is bright.** As I've noted throughout *Beating Bipolar,* people with our mental illness represent every walk of life imaginable. The only difference between those of us floundering and those of us living successfully with this condition lies in our commitment to healing. If you pledge to and actively plot your recovery, you can achieve great things. You can overcome any obstacles in the path to a wonderfully bright future.

RULE 8: **Accept that love is all around you.** When a chronic mental illness is battering your body and abusing your mind, sometimes it's difficult to appreciate the good in the world. Your brain is clicking so fast that you can't see what surrounds you. You can't appreciate that you can care about other individuals and they can care about you. A great tragedy of bipolar disorder is that people feel isolated when they don't need to be isolated. Every day, when I look into Jen's beautiful blue eyes or Tyler's sweet, cherubic face, I know how special it is to feel love. I'm confident that bipolar individuals have the same capacity as other people to express affection. We are divinely connected and at peace with the world around us when we give and receive love.

RULE 9: **Show compassion to family and friends.** Make it your mission in life to tell people how much you care about them. All too often we're so caught up in our bipolar disorder that we don't treat others well, let alone acknowledge how much we love them. I admit that in my own life, I spent years in conceit and annoying behavior. I was terrible to be around. But now I'm acutely aware of how much I love, respect, and appreciate my family and friends. They hear it regularly. When you're loving and gracious, you warm people's hearts.

RULE 10: **Believe and hope.** Dealing with any mental illness is rough—no question about it. Coming to grips with bipolar disorder sometimes takes the patience of Job and the strength of Samson. You have to demonstrate insight and steel in dealing with your condition.

But you also have to believe in your heart and gut that you can get beyond it. No matter how you define hope, it's key to your recovery. Whether it's faith in your ability to change all things or faith that God answers all prayers, hope is a commodity you want in your inside pocket.

One Final Note

The key in handling bipolar disorder is to bring together all of the resources necessary to control your mental illness. It's important to remember that as bleak as your disease seems at times, all is not lost. This is not a terminal illness, unless you allow it to be life threatening. You may be in pain. You may feel isolated and alone. You may even want to give up. But there's good reason to have hope. There's good reason to rise to the occasion. There's good reason to bring your internal "A" game to your recovery. When you turn the corner on this mental illness, you'll be surprised by the adventures that await you. Life will be worth living again!

●　　●　　●

CHAPTER 10

FINDING REBIRTH AND NEW ADVENTURES

WHEREVER YOU ARE on the road to recovery, I hope the journey is becoming clearer to you. Sometimes it's not easy to connect the dots on the map of your life. You don't see how everything fits together. I pray that when you look back on the events of the past, you'll see the positive amid the negative. You'll appreciate that every stop along your path has had meaning and purpose—yes, even bipolar disorder. I believe that once you face the biggest challenges related to your mental illness, you can refocus on healthier, good times. You can appreciate your journey as a new beginning.

I like to think of my bipolar recovery as a spiritual renewal. Many Christian denominations teach that people are *born again* when they accept and recommit to a personal Savior. Their life begins anew. I don't believe you have to be a religious person to appreciate the concept of starting over. Those of us with bipolar disorder have the opportunity to pursue a dynamic life, freed from the frustrations and darkness of the past. I know it's sometimes difficult to let go of old patterns. I talk to people all the time who are in bad or abusive relationships. Yet they're so fearful of either living alone or trying to extricate themselves from the situation that they're locked in place. They've become too comfortable with the past to move away from it.

As bipolar individuals, we're often similarly challenged. It seems easier to stay put than to exert the energy and self-reflection required to move forward. But when you commit to complete healing, you have the chance to make a dynamic fresh start. It doesn't matter if it happens today, tomorrow, or months from now, even though sooner is always better than later. When you're open to recovery and renewal, you can be whole in mind, body, spirit, and heart. Life no longer has its limitations. Instead the future holds untold potential. But how do you successfully tap into that exciting resource we call the world? By embracing your past, opening your mind to the possibilities for the future, and stepping out of your comfort zone, you can finally live your dreams!

Embrace the Past

Memories are tricky. They can be ugly reminders of past pain or fond recollections of wonderful, happy events. As a bipolar survivor, you likely have a mixed bag, maybe even too many of the former and not enough of the latter. In coming to grips with your disorder, you can use memories to take inventory of your life. I know it's difficult to retrace the past. It's not so simple to close your eyes and recall what's happened months or years ago. If you're climbing out of a mental hole, you want to be as far away as possible from the chasm's darkness. But your memories contain many great lessons. I've recognized over time that my reminiscences are a limitless reserve of teachable moments. Whether they contain pain, anger, or disappointment, I don't fear the bad recollections any longer. I embrace them for the truths I can learn from them. They remind me of where I've been and how far I've come in turning my life into something beautiful and worthwhile. They give me great satisfaction.

They're also wonderful reminders of the people who have traveled with us in the past. I recall how my mother dedicated much of her life to helping me when I was first struggling to regain sanity. She never gave up until she found a doctor with a solution that would work for me. In the meantime, it was difficult for her to raise a child with bipolar. I didn't take very well to discipline, especially during my manic episodes. But she kept me focused on structure and rules. More important, she never gave up, no matter how belligerent I became. Nor did any other friends and family members who rallied again and again for my recovery.

Today we have a very tight relationship. Just as my mother has listened to me over the years, I've learned, as an adult, to listen to her. It's a privilege when you can have that kind of relationship with a parent. She's a terrific therapist who connects on a deep emotional level with people. I've learned much by just observing and talking to her. The two of us often commiserate about treatment tools and lessons we've learned from our practices and professional experiences. I have similar supportive relationships with my father and stepfather. Together they've helped me develop both personally and professionally. I can go to them for advice on just about everything, from investing to general tips about life.

Even though my memories are fraught with ugly moments, they're laced with good things about the good people in my life, too. They've helped me move beyond where I was yesterday to where I am today.

Open Your Mind: It's a New Way to Think

In the inspirational movie *The Way*, actor Martin Sheen plays Tom Avery, an irascible ophthalmologist living a pretty predictable life until his brilliant son (played by Sheen's own real-life son Emilio Estevez) throws him a curve. He drops out of his doctoral program to trek the *Camino de Santiago,* or Way of St. James, the famed Catholic pilgrimage through the French Pyrenees to the Cathedral of Santiago de Compostela in Galicia, Spain. Avery doesn't understand his son's desire to experience this adventure or be a citizen of the world . . . that is, until a tragic turn of events—the unexpected death of his son—puts him on the ancient spiritual trail. Although Sheen's character sets out for France to retrieve the young man's remains, he decides instead to honor him by finishing the mission. It's during that pilgrimage that Avery experiences his own profound life-affirming transformation. He learns that there's a difference between "the life we live and the life we choose to live."

Are you ready for the life you choose to live? Hopefully so. Hopefully, you're eager to craft something very special. Perhaps that means opening your mind to new people, new cultures, new customs, new beliefs, and, of course, new experiences. When I lived in New York City, I worked with the homeless. In the beginning, I thought it would be miserable. I couldn't imagine how an entire class of people could live on the fringes. But I learned very quickly that despite being saddled with a spate of complicated issues—bipolar disorder, alcoholism, drug addictions, emotional problems, schizophrenia, and trouble finding work—these people still remained positive in the most challenging situations.

Although some of them eventually found jobs and places to live, many others continued to survive on the streets. Yet they formed a strong sense of community. They forged friendships. They were kind, happy, and brimming with positivity. I learned many lessons about life from those men and women. Even when circumstances are tough, you don't have to give up. You can not only survive but also do it with a good attitude and sense of appreciation. With no clean clothes or a place to shower, they reveled in the simple joys of life: a soup-kitchen meal, a shelter bed, and even a bag of snacks.

I still tear up at the memory of people with no means of visible support holding hands before a free church meal and reciting the Lord's Prayer. At some point in the past, they had learned the iconic words:

Our Father who art in heaven, hallowed be thy name.
Thy kingdom come. Thy will be done on earth, as it is in heaven.
Give us this day our daily bread. And forgive us our debts,
as we forgive our debtors. And lead us not into temptation,
but deliver us from evil. For thine is the kingdom and the
power and the glory forever.
Amen.

No matter how dark it is, you can still find a sliver of light. No matter where your life is, you can still help and encourage others while being empowered by them. By opening your mind and heart, you also open a new chapter. Imagine the new story it might hold!

Go for It

My grandmother is an amazing figure. As they say in certain circles, she marches to her own drummer. Grandmother grew up in Pittsburgh, but chose a path that took her far from her traditional Jewish roots. When she wasn't raising her own family, she pursued an eclectic life, living in far-flung places, from Miami to the Middle East. Her résumé read like a playbill: belly dancer, psychic healer, comedienne, club promoter, and rock star. Hallelujah Bangkok (yes, that was her handle) performed in venues from Los Angeles to Ibiza, Spain. I often find it funny that the same woman whose musical repertoire included "She Was a Hooker" also met the Dalai Lama in her travels.

That was Grandmother. She was an unconventional, one-of-a-kind woman who taught me many lessons about fulfilling dreams and being open to new experiences. Because of her, I don't want to be like the successful doctor I just met who, at age 60, was already lamenting, "Is that all there is?" Of course, that's not all there is if you fill your life with meaning and adventure. I want to be like my grandmother, always looking for new places, people, and experiences.

When Jen and I decided to move to California, it was the culmination of a dream I had held for years. When I was first diagnosed, it was risky to think that I could live outside New York City. How could I venture so far from home? But when the opportunity presented itself, Jen and I were comfortable enough with my recovery to go for it. She wasn't as comfortable, however, about the road trip I suggested we take to the West Coast. After I encouraged her to be open to the experience, she finally agreed. It was a magical, awesome adventure, filled with many diversions and fun stops. Because she stepped out of her comfort zone and enjoyed the ride, we both have great memories of crisscrossing the states.

I've counseled many clients who have made their recovery a springboard for adventure. Once they became healthy and confident, they stepped out of their comfort zones and embraced life: different sights, different sounds, different experiences. Whether pursuing an old dream or an unexpected new one, they're living the lives they want to live, even with bipolar.

- Paul came to me feeling very depressed. He had been diagnosed with bipolar after losing several relationships with women who recognized and were frightened by his mood swings. We worked together for 18 months, until he finally understood some of the underlying issues—including his father's drug addiction—that were driving his emotional problems. When he was finally on the road to recovery, he shared that he had been saving $10,000 to take his dream trip of a lifetime down the Amazon River. Paul took that trip, and besides spying on exotic animals and swimming in tropical streams, he met a beautiful woman who is now his wife.

- Stephanie was completely confused as to what she wanted to do with her life. She had dropped out of college and was grieving her mother's death from brain cancer, when I first started working with her. I helped her sort through the many issues related to her depression, especially the final, sad reality of her mom's death. Even though Stephanie had to work through much sadness, when she was finally emotionally ready, she realized that her mom would want her to finish college. She went back and did very well. After graduation, Stephanie even joined the Peace Corps, traveling to Africa, where she met many new friends while helping children.

- Evan was a great athlete, whose dream was to become a division I college basketball player. But then tragedy struck. His father, Walt, died on a business trip to Israel. Evan was devastated. He lost interest in basketball. For a time his family didn't know how he'd survive the loss. I worked with him for many months to help him get his emotional life back in order. Finally

Evan went back to the sport that he loved, practicing twice as hard as he had in the past. In the end, he earned a full scholarship to a top basketball school. Since 43 was Walt's age at his death, Evan chose to wear the number on his jersey. It was a gesture from the heart to his best friend and coach: his dad!

Whether your adventures take you to faraway places or bring you closer to home, know that your time on Earth is a gift. Every day that you're here, you have the potential to gain wisdom. I feel confident today that I can turn any obstacle, problem, or source of pain into a positive. Yet I still get frustrated, lose my cool, and sometimes want to give up. But when that happens, it just casts a light on the challenges I have yet to overcome in my search for success. Every adversity helps me fine-tune my intuition and increases my resolve to live more fully on my road to recovery. Every day that you're open to change, you have the capacity to learn and to enjoy life. Live it!

Recovery: Spotting the Road Signs

How do you recognize true recovery? When you're on the road to good health, there can be many dips, curves, and detours. Obviously, the experience with bipolar illness is different for each of us. How you manifest your symptoms and react to your treatment is unique to *you*. How much you resist progress is your unique cross to bear. Yet there are certain markers along the roadway that indicate you're making real progress. You should rejoice when you pass them and let them propel you forward. Here are some road signs:

— **You accept your diagnosis and are at peace with your bipolar.** Many of us hope against hope that the psychiatrist was wrong. Even when all the evidence points to a totally dysfunctional life, it couldn't possibly be a mental illness driving us. Isn't it normal to hear voices? Doesn't the television talk to everyone or the refrigerator listen in on all of our conversations? They did for me! I was convinced that the picture tube in my father's apartment was inviting me directly, "Blake, please come to City Hall." What I was supposed to do there was a mystery, but it was a command all the same. Similarly, I was so enamored of the idea that secret devices were hidden in the refrigerator that I unloaded every item in the middle of the night to find them. Not surprisingly, my dad grew concerned. At the time, I couldn't divine reality to save my sanity. Today, I chuckle painfully at the absurdity of it all. That's because I've accepted my disease and am willing to work with and around it. When you're able to admit that your illness is part of who you are and that you need to control it, you've turned a major corner in your life.

— **You're taking a measured approach to your healing.** Someone on the road to recovery realizes that making deliberate choices is the only way to achieve long-term progress. We're no longer looking for the quick fix, even if it's still a challenge. It's against my nature to take small and slow steps in *anything* I do, so the idea that I'd have to work long and hard for complete healing was anathema to me. I couldn't just leap forward without strategizing about what might work for long-term stability. But I recognized that a measured approach gave me the best possible chance for healing. By giving myself time, I became more comfortable with my thought patterns. I learned the importance of sleep in staving off my mania. I understood that not eating correctly was altering my moods and risking my mental health. I acknowledged that I'd have to rebuild my self-confidence by investing in good judgment. Most of all, I accepted that a measured approach pays off on the road to healing.

— **You're stable and able to deal with life.** No matter how large or small the challenges, you have the presence of mind to know why they're occurring and how to handle them. Bipolar or not, it's normal to be upset and struggle when things don't go your way. It's a fact of life to suffer when you experience great personal or professional loss. Yet someone on the road to recovery knows how to navigate those roadblocks by tapping into his or her strategies and support.

— **You have a positive view of yourself.** You finally understand that you're a worthy individual, deserving of an exciting, productive future. It's hard to feel good when your self-esteem and self-worth have hit rock bottom. But people on the road to recovery have turned the negative self-talk into positive vibrations. They've learned to love themselves, accept their illness, and forgive any past episodes or transgressions. They're enjoying stability because of it.

— **You can take care of yourself.** Too often, people with mental illnesses are so incapacitated that they can't take care of life's little or large basics. They don't maintain their treatment, eat well, or exercise daily. They may not even have the wherewithal to bathe or comb their hair. We've all likely been there. But you know that you're on the road to recovery when you not only function but also multitask. (I've even learned how to smile and dance while brushing my teeth!) When you can hold down a job, stay in school, and still stick to the tasks at hand, you're headed in the right direction.

— **You pride yourself on being productive.** I'm not talking about the kind of untamed frenzy during mania that allows you to clean your house in an hour or write prodigiously for ten hours. I'm talking about feeling fresh, alert, and energized every day to get the most out of work, school, your talents, or just life. I'm referring to the goals you can accomplish and the hay you can make when you're not dragged down by deep depression. You know that you're on the road to recovery when you go to bed each night content that you've accomplished what you set out to do that day.

— **You have friends and know how to be a friend.** Too many of us who suffer bipolar are isolated from the normal interactions of life. Whether it's our behavior that puts people off or underlying insecurities that cause us to withdraw, it's difficult sometimes to connect with non-bipolar individuals. You know that you're on the road to recovery, however, when you can engage in healthy, reciprocal relationships based on common interests and activities. Whether it's with one person or a hundred, when you demonstrate that you can connect beyond just your illness, you have socially arrived!

— **You enjoy life.** It's easy to miss the simple joys of life when you're just going through the motions to get through the day. You know you're on the road to recovery, however, when your moods and emotions don't stand in the way of your activities. You're liberated to laugh and go with the flow. I've learned that even the smallest annoyances are easier to bear, because I won't allow them to ruin my day or disrupt my positive outlook. The traffic jam that drove me to distraction in the past is now just a small detour. Instead of cursing the situation, I turn up the music and actually enjoy being patient. I have learned that life is a wonderful mystery to be lived, not just a series of problems to be solved. In fact, when we're most stressed, life can even make us laugh. Just when I'm walking to an important meeting, all caught up in my serious self, a bird poops on my head. Do I curse the slime or laugh at being the target? I've learned that there's humor and peace in accepting life's unexpected diversions, even if I have to clean up the mess.

— **You embrace the present.** Too often, as bipolar individuals we're overwhelmed by the unknowns of the future or hung up on the consequences of the past. The reality of life, however, is that we only have today. How we structure and handle each 24 hours determines if we're going to grovel in our mental illness or live successfully with it. You know you're on the road to recovery when you've decided to make each day count. You're always mindful of using it productively to create a fantastic life!

— **You recognize that you'd rather be an inspiration than sick!** Too often, we don't appreciate the power we have to help others in addition to ourselves. When you're so caught up in a mental illness, it's easy to have tunnel vision. Nothing is more important than taking care of your bipolar—*nothing!* But when you're on the road to recovery, you understand the realities and joys of overcoming your symptoms. You know that you'll sometimes stumble in reaching your destination: a place of peace, hope, and improved health. But once you're there, you can be an inspiration.

When others see that you're doing well in handling your illness, I'm confident that they'll respond positively to your progress. If they're bipolar sufferers themselves, they might be moved to seek help. If they're part of a support network, they'll be encouraged that those of us with this illness can make successful changes. We can be optimistic forces in their lives, too!

One Final Note

Sometimes it's difficult to imagine a positive, exciting life with bipolar, when life has been so negative and taxing thus far. But I believe we're all imbued with that special spirit that pushes us forward no matter what obstacles are in our way. We don't have to just survive bipolar. We can thrive with it. I often think of the movie *Rocky* when I need inspiration to pursue my own adventurous road with my mental illness. Sylvester Stallone's movie alter ego, Rocky Balboa, had plenty of obstacles in his path as the small, underfinanced, and slightly dim-witted amateur boxer taking on the heavyweight champ. Yet he demonstrated that he could take and deliver the punches without a knockout and win in the end.

Isn't that what we have to do with bipolar disorder? Deliver the punches and win? My mother was told that I would never drive a car, go to college, have a regular job, get married, or have a family. My life would be a group home or psychiatric hospital. But she and I disagreed with that prognosis. Today, I drive a car, am a college graduate, run a practice, and am a happy husband and father. Incidentally, I also live in my own beautiful home.

Like Rocky, people who are recovering successfully from bipolar disorder are indeed champions. We turn setbacks into triumphs. We use every opportunity to build our minds and bodies so that we're strong, focused, and ready for adventure. We don't let this illness knock us out by taking away our goals, dreams, and hopes for a healthy future. Instead, we map a path to victory that includes positive reinforcement, continued growth, and yes, even joy. We embrace every occasion not only to let our light shine, but also to reap the benefits of starting anew. Whether we're born again in the religious sense or born again just as thriving bipolar individuals, we live refreshed, motivated, and fulfilled! That's my wish for you!

●　　●　　●

INTO THE LIGHT, REVISITED

BEATING BIPOLAR IS probably not the last book you'll ever read about your mental illness. In fact, I encourage you to continually educate yourself about your condition so that you'll be better prepared to address it today and aware of what might change in the future.

Miracles happen every day in medicine. I'm not saying that a cure for bipolar disorder is around the corner—far from it. But as scientists shed new light on this mental illness, you'll want to keep up with the breakthroughs, particularly if they involve new therapies that could be a great fit for you. Knowing everything there is to know about your chronic illness is a critical first step in proactively participating in your care. The more information you garner, the more you can contribute intelligently to your treatment. I encourage you to be a scholar!

In terms of beating bipolar, if this book puts you on a path to wellness or reinforces the notion that good things can happen for you, I have accomplished my task. When I conceived of a practical guide about dealing with bipolar disorder, I wanted it to be as positive as possible. Even though I'm very aware of the profound dysfunctions connected to this mental illness—and the challenges of getting treated—I truly believe that you can not only tackle this condition, but also overcome it.

I hope that you return to the book often. Use it as incentive to find the proper mental health team and best plan for your condition. Use it as a resource when you want to get specific with your physician or therapist. Use it as a guide if you need advice for creating a support system or navigating your relationships. Finally, use it as inspiration if you're afraid that you can't forge true success. You *can* transform your situation. In fact, I'm so certain that life can change for the better with this illness that sharing my story was imperative for me. (I'd like to hear yours. Please contact me at: **www.willlisten.com**.)

There's great wisdom in the ancient proverb: "When the student is ready, the teacher will appear." I believe that when you truly want healing from bipolar disorder, you'll be open to the process and resources available to help you. You *will* find them. The fact that you're reading this book says that you're ready for the journey (or that you want someone you know to be on that path). The fact that you're contemplating the message means that you understand the personal responsibility attached to controlling your illness.

Whether you're a sufferer or a supporter, I want you to have the confidence that you can turn the darkness of a mental illness into light. As I've encouraged you throughout this book, be bold in overcoming your challenges, take risks (safe ones, of course) to impact your future, and embrace the fact that you have the power to set and achieve lofty goals. Finally, remember that like a diamond, created by extreme heat and pressure, tremendous forces are forming *you*. You may not appreciate it yet, but the challenges of life and your bipolar disorder are shaping you into a gem of untold value. It's time for you to sparkle in the light!

•　•　•

ENDNOTES

Chapter 1

1. See Depression and Bipolar Support Alliance, "Bipolar Disorder Statistics," http://www.dbsalliance.org/site/PageServer?pagename=about_statistics_bipolar.

2. See American Academy of Child & Adolescent Psychiatry, Bipolar Disorder Resource Center, "More on Bipolar Disorder," http://www.aacap.org/cs/bipolar_disorder_resource_center/more_on_bipolar_disorder.

3. See S. L. Johnson, G. Murray, B. Fredrickson, E. A. Youngstrom, S. Hinshaw, J. M. Bass, T. Deckersbach, J. Schooler, and I. Salloum's paper, "Creativity and Bipolar Disorder: Touched by Fire or Burning with Questions?" in *Clinical Psychology Review*, vol. 32, issue 1: pp. 1–12 (2012).

4. See J. C. Soares and J. J. Mann's paper, "The Functional Neuroanatomy of Mood Disorders," in *Journal of Psychiatric Research*, vol. 31, issue 4: pp. 393–432 (1997).

5. See J. C. Soares and J. J. Mann's paper, "The Anatomy of Mood Disorders: Review of Structural Neuroimaging Studies," in *Biological Psychiatry*, vol. 41, issue 1: pp. 86–106 (1997).

6. See N. Gogtay, A. Ordonez, D. H. Herman, K. M. Hayashi, D. Greenstein, C. Vaituzis, M. Lenane, L. Clasen, W. Sharp, J. N. Giedd, D. Jung, T. F. Nugent III, A. W. Toga, E. Leibenluft, P. M. Thompson, and J. L. Rapoport's paper, "Dynamic Mapping of Cortical Development before and after the Onset of Pediatric Bipolar Illness," in *The Journal of Child Psychology and Psychiatry*, vol. 48, issue 9: pp. 852–862 (2007).

7. See Lundbeck Institute. Bipolar Disorder: Aetiology, "What Happens in the Brain?" http://www.brainexplorer.org/bipolar_disorder/Bipolar_Disorder_Aetiology.shtml.

8. See Depression and Bipolar Support Alliance, "Treatment Technologies for Mood Disorders" (2009), http://www.dbsalliance.org/pdfs/Emrg TechsBro09.FINAL.pdf.

9. See J. I. Nurnberger, Jr., and T. Foroud's paper, "Genetics of Bipolar Affective Disorder," in *Current Psychiatry Reports*, vol. 2, issue 2: pp. 147–157 (2000).

10. See note 1 above.

11. See J. B. Potash, J. Toolan, J. Steele, E. B. Miller, J. Pearl, P. P. Zandi, T. G. Schulze, L. Kassem, S. G. Simpson, V. Lopez, D. F. MacKinnon, and F. J. McMahon's paper, "The Bipolar Disorder Phenome Database: A Resource for Genetic Studies," in *The American Journal of Psychiatry*, vol. 164, issue 8: pp. 1229–1237 (2007).

12. See National Institute of Mental Health, "Bipolar Disorder: What Are the Risk Factors for Bipolar Disorder?" http://www.nimh.nih.gov/health/publications/bipolar-disorder/what-are-the-risk-factors-for-bipolar-disorder.shtml.

13. See G. S. Leverich and R. M. Post's paper, "Course of Bipolar Illness after History of Childhood Trauma," in *The Lancet*, vol. 367, issue 9516: pp. 1040–1043 (2006).

14. See National Alliance on Mental Illness, "Bipolar Disorder: Symptoms, Causes, and Diagnosis," http://www.nami.org/Content/NavigationMenu/Mental_Illnesses/Bipolar1/Symptoms,_Causes_and_Diagnosis.htm.

Chapter 2

1. See National Alliance on Mental Illness, "What Is Bipolar Disorder?" http://www.nami.org/Content/NavigationMenu/Mental_Illnesses/Bipolar1/Home_-_What_is_Bipolar_Disorder_.htm.

Chapter 3

1. See Depression and Bipolar Support Alliance, Bipolar Disorder Statistics, http://www.dbsalliance.org/site/PageServer?pagename=about_statistics_bipolar.

Chapter 5

1. See G. S. Sachs, A. A. Nierenberg, J. R. Calabrese, L. B. Marangell, S. R. Wisniewski, L. Gyulai, E. S. Friedman, C. L. Bowden, M. D. Fossey, M. J. Ostacher, T. A. Ketter, J. Patel, P. Hauser, D. Rapport, J. M. Martinez, M. H. Allen, D. J. Miklowitz, M. W. Otto, E. B. Dennehy, and M. E. Thase's paper, "Effectiveness of Adjunctive Antidepressant Treatment for Bipolar Depression," *The New England Journal of Medicine,* vol. 356, issue 17: pp. 1711–1722 (2007).

● ● ●

ABOUT THE AUTHOR

Blake LeVine has helped thousands of individuals and families who are dealing with bipolar disorder. He holds a master's degree in social work from Adelphi University and has been in private practice for many years, first as a therapist and currently as a life coach.

As a mental health professional, Blake brings to the table extensive training and experience in working with sufferers of bipolar disorder, depression, addictions, anxiety, and other mental health challenges. He has counseled adult and teenage sufferers and their families in both individual and group situations, in private practice and in psychiatric institutional settings. Beyond focusing on bipolar disorder, he's worked with people who were dealing with a diversity of topics, from brain cancer to foster care and transgender issues.

As a survivor of bipolar disorder, Blake brings a unique perspective to both his clients and audiences who hear his story. An advocate for the rights of bipolar individuals, he speaks frequently to corporate, school, church, and other audiences on the challenges of living with bipolar disorder. He's been featured in various media outlets, including

Dr. Phil, CNN, ABC, Fox, and **Oprah.com,** and on more than 500 radio programs, including a satellite media tour with Dr. Drew Pinsky.

Blake founded Will Listen, a Los Angeles–based health community that provides group support, one-on-one coaching, and social networking to bipolar individuals and their families, as well as survivors of other traumas. His professional goal is to ensure that people who suffer from mental illnesses know that they can get help and achieve normalcy!

For more information about Blake, please contact his office:

6210 Wilshire Boulevard, Suite 305
Los Angeles, CA 90048
213-304-9555
www.willlisten.com

• • •

NOTES

NOTES

NOTES

NOTES

NOTES

NOTES

NOTES

NOTES

NOTES

NOTES

NOTES

We hope you enjoyed this Hay House Insights book. If you'd like to receive our online catalog featuring additional information on Hay House books and products, or if you'd like to find out more about the Hay Foundation, please contact:

INSIGHTS

Hay House, Inc., P.O. Box 5100, Carlsbad, CA 92018-5100
(760) 431-7695 or (800) 654-5126
(760) 431-6948 (fax) or (800) 650-5115 (fax)
www.hayhouse.com® • **www.hayfoundation.org**

● ● ●

Published and distributed in Australia by: Hay House Australia Pty. Ltd., 18/36 Ralph St., Alexandria NSW 2015 • *Phone:* 612-9669-4299 • *Fax:* 612-9669-4144
www.hayhouse.com.au

Published and distributed in the United Kingdom by: Hay House UK, Ltd., 292B Kensal Rd., London W10 5BE • *Phone:* 44-20-8962-1230 • *Fax:* 44-20-8962-1239
www.hayhouse.co.uk

Published and distributed in the Republic of South Africa by: Hay House SA (Pty), Ltd., P.O. Box 990, Witkoppen 2068 • *Phone/Fax:* 27-11-467-8904 • www.hayhouse.co.za

Published in India by: Hay House Publishers India, Muskaan Complex, Plot No. 3, B-2, Vasant Kunj, New Delhi 110 070 • *Phone:* 91-11-4176-1620 • *Fax:* 91-11-4176-1630
www.hayhouse.co.in

Distributed in Canada by: Raincoast, 9050 Shaughnessy St., Vancouver, B.C. V6P 6E5
Phone: (604) 323-7100 • *Fax:* (604) 323-2600 • www.raincoast.com

● ● ●

<u>**Take Your Soul on a Vacation**</u>

Visit **www.HealYourLife.com®** to regroup, recharge, and reconnect with your own magnificence. Featuring blogs, mind-body-spirit news, and life-changing wisdom from Louise Hay and friends.

Visit **www.HealYourLife.com** today!